Of Kings and Prophets

Shapers of the Destinies of Nations

2016

By Dr. Delron Shirley

Cover design by Jeremy Shirley

Table of Contents

Of Kings and Prophets Shapers of the Destinies of Nations 1

God Always Has a Plan and a Man 3

The Heart of the King 19

Lions and Donkeys 27

How Shall We Escape? 39

Halting Between Opinions 45

Elijah and Elisha 51

Believe the Prophets and Prosper 59

Do It Anyway 69

New Testament Kings, Priests, and Prophets 75

The Making of a Christian Nation 85

This teaching manual is intended for personal study; however, the author encourages all students to also become teachers and to share the truths from this text with others. However, copying the text itself without permission from the author is considered plagiarism which is punishable by law. To obtain permission to quote material from this book, please contact:

Delron Shirley
3210 Cathedral Spires Dr.
Colorado Springs, CO 80904
www.teachallnationsmission.com
teachallnations@msn.com

Of Kings and Prophets
Shapers of the Destinies of Nations

The failed American television series Of Kings and Prophets – from which I've stolen the title for this book – was a very loose retelling of the history of ancient Israel. In fact, it is no surprise that the series didn't make it. Much of the plot centered around historical facts that the average viewer would have no knowledge of. For instance, a recurring theme was the Israelites' need for Philistine iron. Only a student of history would understand that the early period of the kings of Israel occurred just at the transition from the Bronze Age to the Iron Age and that the Philistines developed the technology for producing iron long before the Israelites did – giving them a distinct military advantage because of the superior strength of the iron implements over those made of softer bronze. On the other hand, the series was also destined to be scorned by those who have even a slight working knowledge of history and the Old Testament because script introduced – often in leading roles – characters who are not found in biblical or historical texts, rewrote the roles of those figures that are presented in the Bible, Josephus, and the works of other historical writers, and totally shuffled the events of documented history. In essence, the dramatic series took full advantage of the literary principle known as poetic license. It also alienated much of the Christian viewing audience by prefacing each episode with the disclaimer that viewer discretion is advised. Each installment brimmed and overflowed with intrigue, violence, and lust – yes, things that are certainly part of history and the biblical record, but not as blatant and explicit or as ubiquitous as the television episodes depicted.

Although the series managed to stay on the air for only two episodes, it did embody one aspect that holds true to reality in the drama of the Bible: the plot of both episodes powerfully underscored the tension that exists between the two architects of society – the kings and the prophets. Nations, empires, businesses, history, and the future are always shaped by visionaries – and the two most powerful arenas from which visionaries can mold society are religion and politics. Business, the media, education, and all the other seedbeds of influence in a society – no matter how powerfully they channel the destinies of men – find themselves ultimately in the clutches of these two archetypal forces in the quest to order and even control the minds and energies of man.

Let's take our own journey through the biblical record of the birthing, shaping, razing, and reshaping of the nation of Israel to discover afresh the powerful role of the kings and prophets in each step of this journey. As we make this excursion into history, let us keep our eyes and hearts open for lessons to be learned in shaping the future of our own nation.

God Always Has a Plan and a Man

More than just an unseasonable storm, it was as if the cosmos itself were convulsing with howling winds, torrents of rain, deafening claps of thunder, and blinding flashes of lightning. Though not even the elders of the congregation could ever remember more than just a sprinkle of rain at this time of year, the bright blue skies had suddenly ripped open to unleash this phenomenal tempest as a confirmation of the word of the prophet and an attestation of divine displeasure toward the people's insistent demand.

After generations of divine guidance through God-ordained prophets and patriarchs, the people of Israel had dug in their heels as they laid out their demands before Samuel and had drawn the line in the sand as they insisted that he appoint a king to rule over them just like all the other nations that surrounded them. Even though the historical records read like a telephone book as it lists the kings of the city states that had fallen before the army of Israel who marched without the command of a king, the people no longer wanted to march to the beat of a different drum; they wanted to fit into the mold and pattern of all the other nations.

Although Samuel had insisted that they not force his hand, he came to an impasse as the people's insistence grew stronger and stronger and their logic – that he was too old to continue in the role of leadership and that his sons were unworthy candidates to replace him – seemed incontestable. Grabbing for a trump card, the aging prophet begged for divine intervention; however, the Lord answered with the unexpected response.

> Hearken unto the voice of the people in all that they say unto thee: for they have not

3

> rejected thee, but they have rejected me, that I should not reign over them. According to all the works which they have done since the day that I brought them up out of Egypt even unto this day, wherewith they have forsaken me, and served other gods, so do they also unto thee. Now therefore hearken unto their voice: howbeit yet protest solemnly unto them, and shew them the manner of the king that shall reign over them. (I Samuel 8:7-9)

After hearing from God that he was not to take any offense at the people's request because the problem was not a personal affront to his leadership but a rejection of the very governance of God Himself, Samuel returned to the people with one last negotiation.

> This will be the manner of the king that shall reign over you: He will take your sons, and appoint them for himself, for his chariots, and to be his horsemen; and some shall run before his chariots. And he will appoint him captains over thousands, and captains over fifties; and will set them to ear his ground, and to reap his harvest, and to make his instruments of war, and instruments of his chariots. And he will take your daughters to be confectionaries, and to be cooks, and to be bakers. And he will take your fields, and your vineyards, and your oliveyards, even the best of them, and give them to his servants. And he will take the tenth of your seed, and of your vineyards, and give to his officers, and to his servants. And he will take your menservants, and your maidservants, and your goodliest young men, and your asses, and put them to his work. He will take the

tenth of your sheep: and ye shall be his servants. And ye shall cry out in that day because of your king which ye shall have chosen you; and the LORD will not hear you in that day. (I Samuel 8:11-18)

With total disregard for how taxing and unconcerned for the people's needs the monarch might be, the people continued to clamor for the appointment of a king so that they could join the rest of the international community.

So, after locating the one qualified candidate for the throne, Samuel called a solemn assembly to ordain him into the role of king over the people of Israel – a ceremony that was punctuated with the unnatural squall signifying divine displeasure with the people and their stiff-necked rebellion. Fearing for their very lives from the storm's severity, the people pleaded with Samuel to intercede for them. His comforting response was that if they would turn back to God and whole-heartedly serve Him, He would not forsake them because of His own great name's sake and because it actually pleased Him to make Israel His people. However, the prophet concluded his consolation with one final warning that if the people continued to do wickedly, they would be consumed – both the people themselves and the king that they had insisted upon having.

Even though the demand for a king may have seemed like an abrupt punctuation to the leadership of the prophet Samuel, it certainly came as no surprise to anyone who had been carefully tuned in to all that the Lord had been saying to His people throughout the years. As far back as the days of Moses, the Lord had explicitly predicted the day that Israel would be under the dominion of a king. As the people came to the end of their forty years of wandering through the desert, Moses prophesied that when they finally settled in the land that they were to possess they would seek for king to rule over them. (Deuteronomy 17:14) He even went so far as to spell out the regulations that God would impose upon anyone that they should elevate to the position: he could not be a foreigner; he should not maintain a large cavalry; he should not have multiple wives; he should not amass extreme wealth; and he must make his own personal handwritten copy of the Law to read and live by. (Deuteronomy 17:15-20) In verse thirty-six of the enumeration of the blessings and curses listed in Deuteronomy chapter twenty-eight, Moses again specifically mentioned that the people would set a king over themselves and that he, along with the people, would be exiled unto a pagan nation where they would be forced to serve gods made of wood and stone. Even Hannah – Samuel's own mother – foresaw a day when the people would have a king over them (I Samuel 2:10), even though she likely did not realize that his coronation would represent the rejection of the baby she had just given birth to and the God that graced her with that son. (I Samuel 10:19)

But before we go any further with the story of the transition between the leadership of Samuel and the kings that were to replace him, let's do a little time travel to the former days of Israel and see how God directed them up to the day of this horrific thunderstorm.

Of course, we all know that the whole of human history began with Adam and Eve. During the early days of their lives, this primordial couple walked and talked personally with their Creator Himself. This person-to-person communication was abruptly interrupted when our foreparents rebelled by eating the forbidden fruit and were so overcome by guilt and fear that they hid from the presence of the Lord. Most Bible scholars call this original period when Adam and Eve had direct access to God the Dispensation of Innocence because God created Adam and Eve with no consciousness of sin and without what we have come to call "original sin." Through one act of rebellion, humanity was hurled into what Bible teachers call the Dispensation of Conscience in which man was expected to live according to the awareness of good and evil that Adam and Eve received once they tasted the forbidden fruit.

When we stop to look at the flow of events, it is easy to see that there is a very logical progression here. Adam and Eve lived in a world where they knew only good. In fact, the biblical record notes that, at the end of each day of Creation, God reviewed what He had made and determined that it was good. The only exception was that He felt that it was not good that Adam should be alone; however, once He created Eve, God proclaimed that it was very good. In this perfect world in which there was not even a hint of evil, God gave our ancestral foreparents the simple test of having a chance to find out what evil was all about by tasting of the Tree of the Knowledge of Good and Evil. Once they ate of the forbidden fruit and obtained the knowledge of evil as well as the knowledge of good that they already had, God simply expected that they apply the contrasting information they now had and live according to the good they knew and had experienced while shunning the evil that they were now aware of. In other words, they were to live according their awakened consciences. At this point, it is interesting to note that the Living Bible actually translates the name of this tree as the Tree of Conscience. (Genesis 2:19) Unfortunately, man found it impossible to live by this simple rule of not violating his conscience, and this dispensation ended in failure when "God saw that the wickedness of man was great in the earth, and that every imagination of the thoughts of his heart was only evil continually." (Genesis 6:5)

As soon as man proved that he was incapable of following his conscience, God made the next logical step in His dealings with mankind. Although He had seen that the whole of humanity had perverted themselves into pursuing evil rather than good, there was one singular man – Noah – who caught God's attention because he remained a just and perfect man. (Genesis 6:9) With only one righteous man in the entire population, the most reasonable next step was to move into what has been labeled the Dispensation of Human Government in which the few – or sometimes one singular – righteous individual(s) were to govern all the rest of the corrupted and imperfect population. The one simple rule of this dispensation was that the subjects were to not violate the leadership that God had put into place. Unfortunately, men could not follow this simple mandate. Almost as soon as they had come out of the ark, one of Noah's sons discovered his father unclothed in his tent and ridiculed him to the point that it attracted a curse upon all his descendants. In spite of this early failure, God allowed this flawed dispensation to stumble along until the time of Abraham.

At that point, He initiated a new dispensation, known as the Dispensation of Promise because it was based on the covenant promises that God spoke to His loyal servant Abraham. The covenant that God originated included a number of specific promises including the commitment to bless everyone who blessed Abraham and his seed while also cursing everyone who cursed Abraham or his seed. This promise was passed on through the generations until the time of the captivity in Egypt after the Jewish people immigrated there to escape the famine. It doesn't take a lot of creativity to imagine how the scenario must have played out. I can envision that several generations of Israelites continued to repeat the blessing of Abraham as they symbolically transferred the covenant from father to son. Yet somewhere along the line, one of the sons must have looked up to his aged father and scornfully demanded, "What do you mean? *I'll curse those that curse you!* Everyday I'm cursed by the Egyptian taskmasters. Everyday, they whip and beat me. Everyday, they demand that I work like a dog for nothing. God never curses them. He hasn't made us blessed, and He hasn't given us this so-called Promised Land! Why do you waste your breath reciting this old, dead tradition?"

For four hundred years, the Israelites suffered slavery and persecution in Egypt. Their physical afflictions were tragic, but the real horror was in their loss of faith, hope, and vision. Exodus 2:24 states that God heard their groaning and that He remembered the covenant that He had made with Abraham. It was not the people who remembered that they had a promise and a blessing. The whole idea was lost to them. Only God remembered that to these people belonged a special covenant blessing. The whole foundation of the Dispensation of Promise had eroded away as the people failed to continue to believe what God had said to their forefather Abraham.

At that point, God took the next in the series of logical steps in His dealing with the human race by inaugurating the Dispensation of Law. The obvious logic was that since man could not follow his own conscience nor obey the human leaders that God would place in authority, the only reasonable remedy was to explicitly spell out everything that He expected of them. Therefore, God led them to Mt. Sinai where He gave them the all-inclusive Ten Commandments and all the explicit supporting regulations with one simple rule: don't violate the law. Unfortunately, the people – especially the religious leaders who were supposed to be the ones to set the example for the others – wasted no time finding ways to violate the intent of the law while appearing to observe the outward formalities of the regulations. That is, of course, except in the cases when they simply opted to blatantly rebel against the entire system of godly instruction.

At Calvary, God ended the Dispensation of the Law and introduced His ultimate plan of dealing with fallen humanity – the Dispensation of Grace. In this most magnificent move of divine intervention, God defied the whole system of logic that had characterized the step-by-step flow of the relationship of the Divine with His human subjects. In a mindboggling move that is just too much for our human logic and reason, God determined to take His own Son and make Him a substitute for all our human failures, frailties, and rebellion. By executing upon Jesus all the judgment that the human race deserved, God was able to look at humans as if they were no longer guilty or responsible for having violated the regulations of all the previous dispensations.

From biblical prophecies, we are able to understand that this dispensation will last until the Second Coming of Christ, at which point the final episode of the human-divine saga – the Dispensation of the Millennial Rule of Christ – will commence. In this culmination of the dispensations, Jesus Christ will physically occupy a throne in Jerusalem and personally rule the affairs of humankind.

Notice that as we moved through these various dispensations of God's dealings with mankind, there always seemed to be special individuals who were able to hear God's voice in a unique way in each period – Adam in the Dispensation of Innocence and the Dispensation of Conscience, Noah in the Dispensation of Human Government, Abraham in the Dispensation of Promise, Moses in the Dispensation of Law, all believers who are led by the Holy Spirit in the Dispensation of Grace, and Jesus during the Dispensation of the Millennial Rule of Christ. However, since the Dispensation of the Law lasted some fifteen hundred years, God sent multiple individuals as His spokesmen during this period. Let's take a look at how these various representatives interacted with one another and with the people to whom they were to represent God.

Of course, God's number one spokesperson was Moses. In fact, when Moses was dealing with Pharaoh concerning the release of the people of Israel from Egyptian bondage, the Lord said He had made him like a god and his brother Aaron like a prophet. (Exodus 7:1) Beyond this unique positioning that God gave Moses in his mission to Egypt, Exodus 33:11 tells us that Moses also had an ongoing uniqueness in his relationship with the Lord in that they spoke to one another face to face, as a man speaks with his friend. In the New Testament, Jesus called His disciples His friends in John 15:15, "Ye are my friends, if ye do whatsoever I command you. Henceforth I call you not servants; for the servant knoweth not what his lord doeth:

but I have called you friends; for all things that I have heard of my Father I have made known unto you." He said that they were to do His commands, but not as servants who do so out of obligation. Rather, they were to obey as would friends who know the heart of their friend and willingly fulfill his desires simply because of our love and respect for him. Moses had this kind of one-on-one relationship with God in which he knew the Lord well enough to not simply respond with a "Yes, Sir!" when God give him a directive. Of course, every conversation did end with a "Yes, Sir!" but not with the salute that a private would snap back to his sergeant; rather, it was with the warm handclasp that would be shared by two buddies. Unfortunately, no other of God's human representatives seemed to ever attain to this same level of fellowship with Him. In fact, the Lord specifically prophesied that such a man of intimacy with Him would not arise again until the coming of the messiah. (Deuteronomy 18:15, 18:18)

Along side of Moses was Aaron who was appointed as the high priest and the fountainhead from which the entire priestly order was to arise. In God's own words, the significance of Aaron's position was to manifest God's presence among the people, "And I will sanctify the tabernacle of the congregation, and the altar: I will sanctify also both Aaron and his sons, to minister to me in the priest's office. And I will dwell among the children of Israel, and will be their God. And they shall know that I am the LORD their God, that brought them forth out of the land of Egypt, that I may dwell among them: I am the LORD their God." (Exodus 29:44-46) Unfortunately, as we fast-forward through the history of Israel, we will see that the priesthood more often than not failed horribly at this mission. During the days of King Asa, the Spirit of God came upon Azariah the son of Oded declaring, "For a long season Israel hath been without the true God, and without a teaching priest, and without law." (II Chronicles 15:1) In the years of King Ahaz, Urijah the priest followed the wicked king's commands and constructed a pagan altar in the temple. (II Kings 16:11-16) On the other hand, during the reign of King Jehoash, Jehoiada the priest served as his personal instructor in righteousness and initiated the repairs of the temple. (II Kings 12:2-5)

In fact, we can follow the entire history of civilization, not just the story of the Jewish enclave on the shores of the Mediterranean, and discover that organized religion tends to become a close companion – and, in many cases, synonymous – with government.   As I've traveled around the world, I've encountered numerous examples of how organized religion and national governments essentially serve as one and the same. In India, I visited a Bible college run by a friend of mine. Well, I actually only visited the derelict buildings of the college because the campus had been totally vandalized and so severely damaged by Hindu radicals that it was beyond use and likely beyond repair – all of which happened while the local police stood idly by without intervening to protect the school property or even the lives and wellbeing of the students who were attached and beaten during the raid. The same friend told me that his church building had been invaded by a band of Hindu radicals who brought in a Hindu idol and placed it in the sanctuary. When he went to the local officials about the invasion, the constable ruled that since the church was a place of worship it had to be open to all the people of the community and that they could worship as they pleased – even if it meant bringing in their own images and icons. Essentially, the Christians wound up giving the Hindus their nice building and constructing a flimsy shed on the side of the building for their services. I have many friends in Nepal who have been imprisoned because they resisted the former Hindu government and accepted Christianity. Some were arrested simply because a Bible was found in their homes. In countries like Myanmar and Bhutan where Buddhism predominates, I've learned what it means to arrange to meet friends behind closed doors rather than on a public street, to pull the curtains when gathering for worship or Bible study, and to speak softly and with discrete wording – such as referring to the Bible as "my holy book" – that would not incriminate me. When I contacted embassy of Bangladesh to apply for a visa to enter, I received a packet of information about Islamic history and culture along with the actual visa applications. When I landed in the island nation of the Maldives, I was handed a pamphlet listing all the Islamic regulations that I would be expected to adhere to while in their country and was told to read it before the passport control officer would give me an entry stamp. Today, there are more than eighty countries in the world where Islamic sharia law is either the national legal system or is enforced is regions or among the Muslim citizens of the countries. Even in the United States, at least forty-three, and possibly as many as one hundred, court cases in twenty-three states have been decided upon sharia law rather than our own constitution and laws. Moreover, the North Carolina Senate felt it necessary to pass a bill reminding the state's judges that the laws they are to follow are the ones enacted by the US and state governments – not Islam's sharia.

Of course, the history of Christianity is also totally interwoven with the stories governments of the nations in which the organized church has existed. During the times of the Roman Empire, Christians were seen as disloyal citizens when they refused to serve in the army because it required sacrifice to the Roman gods for their protection. There was one legion, however, that was composed entirely of Christians – the Thebam Legion. When Emperor Maximian ordered a pagan sacrifice and required that the legion to not only participate but to also take an oath of allegiance swearing to eradicate Christianity from Gaul, the entire legion refused. Maximian was so enraged that he ordered every tenth man to be killed. When the remaining ninety percent still refused to comply with the order, he again decimated the force. When those still standing refused to recant, the emperor, in a fit of rage, ordered all surviving five thousand four hundred soldiers executed – and the Christians were hacked to pieces. The testimony of these men exemplified the character of the early church who feared man so little because they feared God so much.

In AD 250, Emperor Decius issued an edict forcing all citizens to make yearly sacrifices to the Roman deities and the "divine emperor," forcing the Christians to take a public stance for their faith and in opposition to the government. The government's reaction to their tenacious resistance precipitated in an empire-wide retaliation against the church. In AD 303, Emperor Diocletian issued an edict ordering every citizen to take part in public sacrifice to the pagan gods, the destruction of all church buildings, the imprisonment of church leaders, and the burning of Christian scriptures. February 23, 303, was declared "Terminalia" – the day the pagan world hoped to exterminate all Christianity. Contrary to all logical anticipation, the attempt to eradicate the faith only fostered its growth. Tertullian, an early church leader, summed up the effect of this persecution when he reported, "The oftener we are mown down by you, the more in number we grow; the blood of Christians is seed." However, a dramatic change occurred in AD 312 as Constantine found himself pitted against Maxentius in the Battle of Milvian Bridge for control of the Empire. Just before entering the fray, he reportedly witnessed the sign of a cross in the heavens accompanied by the command, "In this sign conquer." This vision led him to declare himself a Christian and to make it his aim as the new emperor to Christianize the empire. In AD 313 he issued the Edict of Milan that granted freedom of religion to all faiths and in AD 325 he called together the Council of Nicaea that unified the church in doctrine and function within empire. In his attempt to make the empire Christian, Constantine confiscated pagan temples and turned them into Christian churches, placed the clergy on the national payroll, and marched the army through the river as a mass baptism. Unfortunately, when Constantine removed the persecution he replaced it with government sanctions that led the church to depend upon the system rather than God, causing them to lose the one real impetus for genuine mission – the power of the Spirit. When asked how this new-found favor had affected the church, one bishop responded, "We can no longer say as did Peter, *Silver and gold have I none.*" Then, after a reluctant pause, he added, "However, no longer can we say, *In the name of Jesus rise up and walk.*" This interdependence of the church and the state has dominated the history of Europe ever since. In the transition years between the eight and ninth centuries, Emperor Charlemagne – determined to advance the faith by force – declared that conversion be included in the terms of peace for each German tribe that was conquered. In his zeal to punish those tribes that were not willing to accept the rule of the Catholic Church, Charlemagne resorted to extreme measures. Historical records testify that he wiped out whole communities, burned their villages, destroyed their crops, and killed as many as forty-five hundred men, women, and children in one day. In Scandinavia, a different pattern emerged between the church and the state. Although he bitterly opposed the faith, the king of Denmark was convinced to allow the building of two churches and the introduction of the faith to the populace of his nation. From there, the fortune of the church varied from reign to reign as subsequent kings either embraced or rejected the church. The Christian faith came to Norway because of political advantages rather than due to genuine religious conviction. When Christianity was introduced to the British Isles in AD 596, King Ethelbert refused to receive the message of the missionaries until his wife became a Christian and persuaded him to convert. Upon the king's profession of faith, Christianity became the official religion of the country and ten thousand new converts were baptized in one day.

Essentially, Europe was totally dominated by the Catholic Church. During the Age of Exploration when men like Christopher Columbus, Vasco de Balboa, Ferdinand Magellan, and Vasco de Gama were braving the high seas to discover new worlds, they first had to have permission and blessings from the popes before they could weigh their anchors. Popes appointed kings, and kings appointed popes. That is until Martin Luther slipped out on the night of October 31, 1517, to nail the Ninety-five Theses on the door of the Cathedral of Wittenberg – setting off the sparks that eventually raged into the blaze of the Protestant Reformation. However, the ensuing wars and restructuring of the nations and churches did little to break the ties between church and state – they simply realigned, and likely strengthened, the unions. Now, instead of the nations being married to one church, there were nations that divorced themselves from Catholicism simply to establish their own new denominations to wed. As the dust of the battles of the Reformation settled, a new scene in Europe began to appear – nations that were even more strictly aligned with the Lutheran or Presbyterian churches than they had been to the Catholic Church before the conflict. Laws were based on church doctrine and national taxes paid for church building and the salaries of the clergy.

Having used the metaphor of marriage, we can't leave this topic without at least mentioning the rise of the Anglican Church, which broke away from Rome in 1534 because the pope would not permit King Henry VIII to divorce his wife and remarry. As a result, the English Parliament simply declared that England would have its own church with the king as its supreme head – proclaiming that the English desired to be independent from continental Europe religiously and politically.

Jumping back into our time machine, let's rewind history back to the days of the Old Testament. Our first port of call will be Egypt during the time of Joseph. There is one interesting fact that we need to consider – an aspect of the story that otherwise might remain an unexplained mystery without the perspective that we've gained from our current study of history. In Genesis chapter forty-seven, we read the story of how Joseph bought all the land of Egypt from the inhabitants during the seven years of famine; however, verse twenty-two notes that there was one exception – the land of the priests. Verse twenty-six follows up that the previous landowners were then to serve as sharecroppers who were to relinquish twenty-percent of their yield to the pharaoh – except for the priests. The perplexing question would be why Joseph made such exclusions for the pagan priests. The simple answer is that they were in control of the government. Even though Joseph was second in command to the pharaoh himself, he still had to work within the system – and that system, as we have seen throughout all human history, was a marriage of the religion and the government. The next stop that I'd like to schedule for our time machine would be Babylon during the time of Daniel. When Daniel and his three companions (Hananiah, Mishael, and Azariah) were chosen to be trained as Chaldeans, the first order of business was to change their names to Belteshazzar, Shadrach, Meshach, and Abednego. The reason behind this name change was significant because their original names contained references to the God of Israel, but their replacement names were to give recommendation to the gods of the Babylonians. There was strategic significance to this move in that the Chaldeans were the advisors to the royal family – and it just wouldn't look right for the heads of the government to receive counsel from anyone whose very name decried the religious system that permeated the political system. What we see in these two examples is a foreshadowing of the difference between the priest who represents organized religion that meshes with the king who represents the government and the prophet who represents the voice of God that speaks autonomously – free from both king and priest.

Early on in this chapter, we made the point that Aaron – symbolizing the role of organized religion – was to manifest God's presence among the people, "And I will sanctify the tabernacle of the congregation, and the altar: I will sanctify also both Aaron and his sons, to minister to me in the priest's office. And I will dwell among the children of Israel, and will be their God. And they shall know that I am the LORD their God, that brought them forth out of the land of Egypt, that I may dwell among them: I am the LORD their God." (Exodus 29:44-46)

When the priest fails, the prophet must arise!

The Heart of the King

After Moses, Aaron, and Moses' personal protégé Joshua passed off the scene, Israel went through a transitional period in which God raised up a series of men and one woman as judges to deliver and lead the nation. One interesting observation about the period of the judges is that the chronicler of this period of history on at least four different occasions made reference to the fact that there was no king in Israel at this time and that as a result the people did as they pleased. (Judges 17:6, 18:1, 19:1, 21:25) The rest of the study of the nation's history will confirm that simply having a king in place didn't seem to deter the people from continuing to do as they felt justified in their own eyes. The concluding figure of this epoch was our friend Samuel who called that off-season deluge upon the land. Not only did Samuel serve as a judge (implied in I Samuel 8:5), in the role of a priest (I Samuel 2:11), and as a prophet (I Samuel 3:20), he also anointed the first two kings of the nation – Saul (I Samuel 10:24) and David (I Samuel 16:13).

Only two years into his reign, King Saul found himself at odds with the prophet because he became impatient while waiting for Samuel to come to perform a sacrifice before the army went out to battle against the Philistines. Watching his recruits begin to fall from rank, the king was concerned that his numbers would dwindle too low to engage the enemy if he postponed the attack any longer; therefore, he took it upon himself to make the offering rather than waiting for Samuel to arrive. (I Samuel chapter thirteen) However, the ultimate breach between the king and the prophet came when Samuel directed Saul to mete out retribution against the Amalekites for their attacks against the people of Israel as they came out of Egypt. By making the decision to save the best of the flocks and herds and to spare the king, Saul blatantly defied the orders of the prophet, and Samuel responded by declaring that he would never again minister to the king and that God would soon remove him from his position. (I Samuel 15:26) Afterwards, Saul was not able to hear from God through any means – dreams, Urim, or prophet (I Samuel 28:6) and eventually turned to witchcraft in his quest for guidance (I Samuel 28:7).

Samuel's second king was a radically different story. Yes, David did have some failures – in fact, such very serious and glaring catastrophes that many other men would not have been able to regain their footing had they encountered events of similar magnitude. But unlike Saul, there was something about David that made him get up and keep going after each downfall. The first failure that comes to mind immediately when we think of King David is his moral failure with Bathsheba. The eleventh chapter of II Samuel records the story of how David spied her one evening as she bathed on the roof of the neighboring villa. The episode exposes a serious flaw in David's moral fiber. An old saying tells us that we can't stop the birds from flying above our heads, but we can stop them from building a nest in our hair. David was guilty of not shooing away the birds of lustful thoughts before they had a chance to build a nest in his heart. James 1:14-15 tells us that sin is the result of temptation that is the product of lust. James adds that we are "drawn away by our own lust," suggesting that lust is not so much an external temptation as it is an internal motivation. At the first sighting of the maiden washing herself, King David could have quickly turned away and gone back to bed; however, he chose rather to take a second glance, then a longer more intense look, then a stare, then a gaze before he returned to bed – unfortunately, he was not alone when he finally fell asleep again. David had followed the predictable pattern of allowing a temptation to take root inside his heart and develop into a lustful attitude that eventually resulted in acted out sin. David's most famous flaw was his moral failure with Bathsheba – the outgrowth of his lack of personal discipline over his thought life.

Intimately linked with his moral failure with Bathsheba was his gross failure in the arena of loyalty as demonstrated in his dealings with Uriah, Bathsheba's husband. Uriah, one of David's most able and dependable warriors, was away at battle at the time of the incident between his wife and the king. When David learned that Bathsheba was pregnant, he called her husband home from the front in order to make it appear that Uriah was the father of the child. The scriptures record a remarkable story of Uriah's loyalty to the troops when he refused repeated offers to be with his wife, stating that he could not enjoy privileges that his men were being denied. What a picture of contrast between Uriah who refused his legitimate benefits in respect for his suffering troops and the king who indulged in not only his legitimate privileges but extended into illegitimate pleasures while his men suffered deprivation at the front. The end of the story is that when David could think of no other solution, he had Uriah killed and married Bathsheba with the hopes that no one would count to see if there were nine months between the royal wedding and the birth of the baby. In the most heinous deed of his career, David sent his loyal servant back to the front bearing his own death warrant. It was only when the prophet Nathan exposed the sin (II Samuel 12:7) that David was willing to admit and address his flaws.

Yet, his faults against Bathsheba and Uriah were not nearly as serious as his failure toward God. David himself realized this when he framed the prayer recorded in Psalm fifty-one in which he repented for these atrocities. In verse four, David says, "Against You and You alone have I sinned," indicating that he realized that the incidents involving adultery with Bathsheba and the murder of Uriah were only outward manifestations of the inward sin he had committed against God Himself. Apparently, David had slipped away from the intensity in his fellowship with and worship of God. He ends the psalm with a renewal in his commitment to worship, suggesting that he realized that his basic flaw was failing to pursue after the heart of God. When he spoke of his sin against God, David's word for "sin" can be interpreted with either of two meanings – "to miss the mark" or "to rebel." In essence, he had missed the mark by failing to intently follow after God's presence resulting in a rebellion against His ways. "I said, LORD, be merciful unto me: heal my soul; for I have sinned against thee." (Psalm 41:4)

But David's failure toward God can also be seen as a failure toward himself. Through this sin, David came dangerously close to experiencing the Holy Spirit's departing from his life because of his rebellion against God and society. The prayer he prayed for restoration after these heinous sins reveals how close he had come to slipping over the edge. But first, let's take a quick look at exactly what happened inside David's soul during this ordeal. "Then will I go unto the altar of God, unto God my exceeding joy: yea, upon the harp will I praise thee, O God my God." (Psalm 43:4) "God, my exceeding joy" – what a wonderful way to express our relationship with God! To David, the Lord was not a source of joy or his reason to be joyful – but joy itself. Additionally, it was not what God did for David, or even the fact that they had a relationship, that made him joyful; it was God Himself that was the Psalmist's joy. On top of all this, God was not only David's joy; he was his exceeding joy – joy beyond measure. Yet David's life was not always characterized by joy. In the Psalms, he often speaks of sorrow and anguish. (Psalm 13:2, 38:17, 39:2, 55:10, 107:39, 116:3, 119:143) At one point, he even described his internal agony as so severe that he said that his tears figuratively made his bed to swim. (Psalm 6:6) In Psalm 38:3, he mourns, "There is no soundness in my flesh because of thine anger; neither is there any rest in my bones because of my sin." In Psalm 32:3, he laments that his very bones grew old through his "roaring" (loudly vocalized agony) all day long. In what seems to be a contradiction of terms, he says that the reason behind these internal roarings is his external silence. His silence was his refusal to confess the sins he had committed during this snowballing escapade. (verses 1-2) His silence about his sin filled him with sorrow, causing him to roar with agony and float his bed with his tears. His whole problem was that he was cut off from Joy Himself. His reconciliation prayer describes how he renewed his relationship with God and was restored to joy. "Make me to hear joy and gladness; that the bones which thou hast broken may rejoice...Cast me not away from thy presence; and take not thy holy spirit from me. Restore unto me the joy of thy salvation; and uphold me with thy free spirit." (Psalms 51:8, 11-12)

When Nathan the prophet confronted David after the Bathsheba incident, he reminded the king that God had prospered him with incredible gifts and then went on to declare that God was actually willing to give David even more. But in the middle of all this prosperity and increase, David desired to have – and took – the one thing that God was not willing to give him, his neighbor's wife. It is interesting that the story is explicit in depicting Bathsheba's residence as being so close to David's home that he could see her clearly from his terrace. In other words, she was literally his neighbor. Thus, he defied the commandment against coveting one's neighbor's wife in a literal sense as well as in the figurative sense in which the passage is intended. (Exodus 20:17) "And I gave thee thy master's house, and thy master's wives into thy bosom, and gave thee the house of Israel and of Judah; and if that had been too little, I would moreover have given unto thee such and such things." (II Samuel 12:8)

The significance of the prophet Nathan in the life of King David is that the prophet served as a friend and advisor to the king. Yes, he boldly accused David and didn't "pull any punches" when dealing with him; however, there was a relationship between the two men that allowed this kind of confrontation without conflict. The underlying principle here seems to be in the heart attitude of the king himself. There is one characteristic that seemed to stand out in David's life that could have made the difference between him and any others who lacked this quality, and we find it identified in the very first story that we read about him as a mere lad – the criteria that determined his selection for the throne of Israel. After Samuel had surveyed the seven older sons of Jesse without finding a worthy candidate, the Lord revealed to him that he was looking at the wrong score card when evaluating his options. God made His point that the heart of the matter was actually the matter of the heart.

> But the LORD said unto Samuel, Look not on his countenance, or on the height of his stature; because I have refused him: for the LORD seeth not as man seeth; for man looketh on the outward appearance, but the LORD looketh on the heart. (I Samuel 16:7)

David obviously understood that this was his key to success and determined to keep his heart in a perfect relationship with his God. "I will behave myself wisely in a perfect way. O when wilt thou come unto me? I will walk within my house with a perfect heart." (Psalms 101:2) Even after he sinned with Bathsheba and had her husband killed, the king's prayer was that God would re-establish his heart before Him. (Psalms 51:10) Consequently, the New Testament characterized David as being a man after God's own heart. (Acts 13:22) This heart attitude allowed him to be able to hear the words of the prophet and allow them to get him back on tack rather than to rebel against the prophet's message and blatantly follow his own course – unlike Saul who refused to word of the prophet and was rejected from his position because he had developed a heart attitude of arrogance and pride. (I Samuel 15:17)

This is not to say that David was totally "off the hook." In spite of David's repentance, the prophet Nathan declared that the sword would never depart from David's house as a punishment for his sins. (II Samuel 12:10) As a result of this sin, David was never able to know peace from his conflicts and conquests, a factor that kept him from being able to fulfill one of the greatest of his dreams – that of building a temple in Jerusalem to house the Ark of the Covenant. (I Kings 5:3; I Chronicles 22:8, 28:3) The impact of this story is that David had drawn up all the plans for the temple and collected billions of dollars' worth of gold, silver, and building materials for this project, but he was forbidden from initiating the actual construction. (I Chronicles 15:12, 22:14, 28:11-21, 29:2-3) His sin of internally allowing his heart to be turned away from God resulted in David's being disqualified from the one project that would externally demonstrated his passion for Him.

One other prophet who spoke into the life of King David was Gad the seer, who gave the king three options concerning the consequences he was to face after he numbered the fighting forces of Israel. (I Chronicles 21:9) Although we see many examples of the taking of a census as a way to determine the nation's military strength, this act on the part of David was a giant step backwards from his previous declaration of faith in God alone, "Some trust in chariots, and some in horses: but we will remember the name of the LORD our God." (Psalm 20:7) When Gad offered the king three options – three years of famine, three months of destruction before his enemies, or three days of the sword of the Lord – David immediately opted for the sword of the Lord with the explanation, "Let me fall now into the hand of the LORD; for very great are his mercies." (I Chronicles 21:13) This conclusion demonstrated that the intervention of the seer had brought King David back to his dependence upon and trust in the Lord. In this king's life, the prophets served to draw out best of king – his heart relationship toward God. Because of this one quality, David became the "gold standard" by which all other kings were measured. (I Kings 8:66, 9:4, 9:5, 11:4, 11:6, 11:12, 11:13, 11:32, 11:33, 11:34, 11:36, 11:38, 11:39, 15:3, 15:4, 15:5,

15:11; II Kings 8:19, 14:3, 16:2, 18:3, 19:34, 20:5, 20:6, 21:7, 22:2; II Chronicles 7:17, 7:18, 13:5, 17:3, 21:7, 21:12, 28:1, 29:2, 34:2, 34:3) In fact, it was almost as if he were the only king that God actually recognized as legitimate.

Lions and Donkeys

In Saul we saw an example of the king working in opposition to the prophet; while in David we saw a case a king working in cooperation with the prophets of God. With Solomon, Israel's third king, we see another aspect of visionary leadership. Other than the involvement of the prophet Nathan in assuring that Solomon rather than his brother Adonijah was installed in place their father David (I Kings 1:22), we do not see any prophetic counsel during the reign of Solomon. In fact, extra-biblical literature actually lists the king himself as a prophet. The Talmud lists Solomon as one of the forty-eight Jewish prophets, and the Quran considers him a major prophet of the Islamic faith. Indeed, Solomon was a man of such significant personal encounter with God that – for the most part – he likely didn't need the input from a prophet. In addition to all the personal wisdom and insights that the Lord granted to the king, Solomon had two direct individual encounters with the Lord and one occasion in which the Lord spoke specifically – and possibly even audibly – to him.

One of the first things that Solomon did upon ascending to his father's throne was to go to high place at Gibeon to sacrifice and seek the Lord's guidance for his rule. In a genie-in-the-bottle-like dream, the Lord appeared to the young king and offered him a write-you-own-ticket deal to ask for anything that he could imagine. Noting that his father had walked before the Lord in truth and in righteousness and uprightness of heart, Solomon confessed that he felt like an unschooled child who didn't know how to even go out or come in among the people he was supposed to lead. He then asked for an understanding heart to be able to rightly judge the people and to be able to discern between what is good and what is bad. God responded that he could have asked for many things – including long life, riches for himself, the lives of his enemies – but he had not asked for anything for himself but rather for the good of his people. Therefore, the Lord promised him all the things that he did not request as well as the wise and understanding heart that he sought. (I Kings 3:3-15)

The second appearance of the Lord came at the dedication of the temple when the Lord declared, "I have hallowed this house...to put my name there for ever; and mine eyes and mine heart shall be there perpetually. And if thou wilt walk before me, as David thy father walked, in integrity of heart, and in uprightness, to do according to all that I have commanded thee, and wilt keep my statutes and my judgments...There shall not fail thee a man upon the throne of Israel. But if ye shall at all turn from following me, ye or your children, and will not keep my commandments and my statutes which I have set before you, but go and serve other gods, and worship them...this house, which I have hallowed for my name, will I cast out of my sight; and Israel shall be a proverb and a byword among all people: And at this house, which is high, every one that passeth by it shall be astonished, and shall hiss; and they shall say, Why hath the LORD done thus unto this land, and to this house?" (I Kings 9:2-9)

Solomon's third visitation came after he had allowed his foreign wives to seduce him into worshipping their pagan gods. In His fury, the Lord spoke vehemently to the king, "Forasmuch as this is done of thee, and thou hast not kept my covenant and my statutes, which I have commanded thee, I will surely rend the kingdom from thee, and will give it to thy servant. Notwithstanding in thy days I will not do it for David thy father's sake: but I will rend it out of the hand of thy son. Howbeit I will not rend away all the kingdom; but will give one tribe to thy son for David my servant's sake, and for Jerusalem's sake which I have chosen." (I Kings 11:11-13) This one prophetic word, spoken explicitly from the mouth of God Himself directly into the ears of the king himself, served as the trigger to the floodgate that released the cascade of prophet-king events that marked Israel's history for the next five centuries.

The narrative in I Kings goes on to add in the following verse that the Lord stirred up an adversary against Solomon, a league between the Edomites and Egyptians. Later in the chapter, we find that another adversary was aroused among the Syrians. Additionally, Jeroboam (who would eventually snatch part of the nation from the hand of Solomon's son) proved himself to be an industrious young man and a mighty man of valor; therefore, Solomon elevated him to a position of authority in the nation, not knowing that he would eventually rise up against the royal family. The next dramatic step in the-prophet-versus-the-king scenario played out as the prophet Ahijah the Shilonite approached Jeroboam outside Jerusalem and – grabbing his brand new tunic – began to rip it into shreds. Handing Jeroboam ten of the twelve pieces of his former vestment, the prophet proclaimed that God intended to rip the kingdom out of the hand of Solomon and take ten of the twelve tribes to make a separate nation under Jeroboam's leadership. The prophet went on to say that, for the sake of His covenant with David and His prophetic determination concerning Jerusalem, God would preserve the city and two tribes under the leadership of the Davidic house. Once Solomon got wind that a subversion might be in the works, Jeroboam was forced to flee into Egypt until the monarch's death. At that point, he returned to Jerusalem to confront the heir to the throne. The scripture does not make it clear as to what Jeroboam's motives were, but his tactic was to approach Rehoboam with a tax-relief proposal. It is possible that Jeroboam could have had totally altruistic motives in suggesting a way for the new king to gain favor with the people and, therefore, preserve unity in the kingdom. However, in that he already had a prophetic word concerning the demise of the national unity, it is likely that Jeroboam had the ulterior motive of forcing the new sovereign's hand so that he could make his own move toward taking the part of the kingdom that had been promised to him. Regardless of the motive, the end result was exactly what we could have anticipated – Rehoboam refused to lessen taxes and actually increased them, forcing the tribes that were away from Jerusalem to rebel while the people in the vicinity of the capital (where all the tax money was flowing into) reaffirmed their loyalty to the Davidic house. The whole scenario flung the door full open for Jeroboam to walk in and take the reins of the ten northern tribes – fulfilling the words of the prophet!

It really doesn't take a student of history or an expert in military strategy to predict what happened next – Rehoboam retaliated by planning an armed attack against Jeroboam. However, the next twist in the plot was certainly not on anybody's radar – a prophet stepped out of the woodwork and totally disarmed the king's plans! According to the narrative in I Kings chapter twelve, the otherwise unknown prophet Shemaiah advised the king not to attack since it would be a fight against his own brethren. Following the command of the prophet, all the troops returned to their houses and did not resist the secession of the northern tribes.

The next wave of the prophet-king interplays unfolds dramatically in chapter thirteen as the fledging northern kingdom made some serious blunders that were to characterize its entire history. Knowing that he would never have the full loyalty of his subjects as long as they continued to travel to Jerusalem to worship, Jeroboam knew that he had to come up with an alternative to temple worship. His plan was to build smaller shrines in the northern kingdom and encourage the people to sacrifice and worship at them rather than to feel obligated to journey all the way to Jerusalem to worship in Solomon's temple. No matter how logical the approach might have seemed humanly, God considered it an immediate abandonment of true worship and an adopting of paganism and idolatry. He, therefore, sent one of His prophets to confront the new king.

This unnamed prophet, known only as "a man of God," was commissioned to go from Judah to the city of Bethel where Jeroboam had set up an altar and to confront the king as he participated in burning incense. His prophecy was to go on and specifically name a child to be born in the family of David generations later who was to destroy the altar and burn human bones upon it. To confirm the validity of his prophecy, the man of God was to call for an immediate sign – that the altar would split apart and that the ashes upon it would pour out upon the ground. When the man of God executed his divine mandate, King Jeroboam pointed toward the prophet, directing his men to arrest him. Miraculously, the king's arm became paralyzed in place so that he could not move it until he begged the man of God to intercede to the Lord for the restoration of the use of his hand. Having seen the altar spontaneously break open at the voice of the prophet and having experienced the paralysis and unfreezing of his own arm, the king invited the prophet to his palace to receive a reward; however, the man of God refused, saying that God had commanded him not to tarry long enough to eat or drink during his journey but to leave town immediately and follow a different route home.

In an incredible turn of events, an old prophet who lived in the area heard of the events and sent his son to invite the man of God to his house. In order to convince the man of God that it was okay for him to come to his house, the old prophet lied by saying that an angel had appeared to him and rescinded mandate about not tarrying during the journey. When the man of God left the prophet's house, he was attacked and killed by a lion. This enigmatic story serves as a warning and an instruction manual for those who might feel called to speak prophetically to their nation. The man of God had a direct command from the Lord, which he fairly readily disregarded when approached by the son of the old prophet with the message that an angel had appeared to his father and repealed the original directive. Although we are certainly to take counsel and direction from the elders in the Body of Christ, we must never trust another's "word from God" above our own unless we already have an uncertainty or uneasiness that would make us question that we fully understood the Lord's word to us. In the case of this man of God, there was no room for such doubt in that everything had happened exactly as he had predicted and there had been a miraculous confirmation of his prophecy when the altar split open and poured out the ashes on the ground. Furthermore, any doubts about his authority would have been totally dispelled when the king's arm was paralyzed. In fact, the man of God was so certain about his mandate from God that he refused the king's dinner invitation; however, the fact that the second invitation came from a supposed prophet made me have second thoughts – the exact thing that Paul warns us against in Galatians 1:8, "But though we, or an angel from heaven, preach any other gospel unto you than that which we have preached unto you, let him be accursed." The second lesson we learn is from the old prophet – even though he lied and endangered the man of God, he was still a prophet in that he interrupted the dinner party to speak a word of doom over the man of God because of his disobedience. The point here is the same message that the Apostle Paul conveyed in I Corinthians 13:9 when he said that we know in part and prophesy in part. The lesson is that even though we can never take the word of any minister as one-hundred-percent infallible, that doesn't disqualify everything he might say. We see the same principle played out in Acts chapter twenty-one when prophetic words were spoken over Paul concerning how he would be arrested in Jerusalem and then the believers went on to say that he should not go to the city so as to avoid the incarceration and following trials. The final lesson in this story comes from the unnatural scenario that the man of God's donkey did not run away when the lion attacked and that the lion killed but did not consume the man of God – depicting how out of order the whole episode was that a man could so clearly hear from

God and deliver such a poignant message to the nation yet be so haphazard with his own life. Unfortunately, many throughout history and in contemporary society who have prophetic messengers that can move nations often wind up "crashing and burning" in their own personal lives.

Let's take minute and go back and examine the prophecy that the man of God delivered. But before we do that there is one observation that we must make in reference to the topic of discussion in the previous chapter. First Kings 13:31 notes that Jeroboam made priests of the lowest of the people, which were not of the sons of Levi; II Chronicles 11:15 makes the story even more disturbing when it adds that these priests were actually appointed to the service of demons. The story goes on to say that he personally was offering sacrifices at the altar when the man of God arrived – in essence, the king had appointed himself as the high priest. What a splendid example of the association of the priesthood and the king – and an even more excellent example of how corrupt such a union can become. The word that the man of God delivered into this perverted situation is undoubtedly one of the most remarkable and most singular prophecies in the Old Testament. It precisely foretold a series of events that would unfold exactly as he spelled them out, but not for three hundred and forty years after the prediction! He even predicted the name of the name of the man who was to bring all these events to pass. (I Kings 13:2) The prophecy came to precise fulfillment as recorded in II Kings 23:15-20 under the rule of Josiah – one of the infrequent examples in the history of Judah when the king and the priests worked together to establish a godly rule in the nation.

Chapter fourteen of I Kings tells an intriguing story of the interaction between King Jeroboam and the prophet Ahijah. When the prince fell ill, Jeroboam sent the queen to inquire of the prophet about the boy's destiny. Even though Jeroboam had refused the word of the man of God who had dramatically confirmed his prophetic utterance with miraculous signs and even though Jeroboam was actively promoting idolatry in the nation, he chose a true prophet of God as his source when he needed a supernatural intervention. Assumedly because of his public promotion of paganism, the king asked his wife to disguise herself and make a secret mission to Shiloh to speak to the prophet. Since Ahijah was blind, there was no real need for the masquerade in trying to fool him; therefore, the ruse was apparently to keep anyone who might discover the purpose of the mission from exposing the king's hypocrisy. Even though the prophet could not see physically, he had perfect spiritual sight – an attribute that resulted in the custom of calling prophets "seers" at this point in history. (I Samuel 9:9) Because of this keen ability of discernment, the prophet knew who was at his doorstep and the purpose of her visit even before he answered the knock on his door. After shocking her by revealing her identity that was doubly hidden – by her disguise and by his blindness – the prophet sent her on her way with more of a message than she had bargained for:

> Go, tell Jeroboam, Thus saith the LORD God of Israel, Forasmuch as I exalted thee from among the people, and made thee prince over my people Israel, And rent the kingdom away from the house of David, and gave it thee: and yet thou hast not been as my servant David, who kept my commandments, and who followed me with all his heart, to do that only which was right in mine eyes; But hast done evil above all that were before thee: for thou hast gone and made thee other gods, and molten images, to provoke me to anger, and hast cast me behind thy back: Therefore, behold, I will bring evil upon the house of Jeroboam, and will cut off from Jeroboam him that pisseth against the wall, and him

that is shut up and left in Israel, and will take away the remnant of the house of Jeroboam, as a man taketh away dung, till it be all gone. Him that dieth of Jeroboam in the city shall the dogs eat; and him that dieth in the field shall the fowls of the air eat: for the LORD hath spoken it. Arise thou therefore, get thee to thine own house: and when thy feet enter into the city, the child shall die. And all Israel shall mourn for him, and bury him: for he only of Jeroboam shall come to the grave, because in him there is found some good thing toward the LORD God of Israel in the house of Jeroboam. Moreover the LORD shall raise him up a king over Israel, who shall cut off the house of Jeroboam that day: but what? even now. For the LORD shall smite Israel, as a reed is shaken in the water, and he shall root up Israel out of this good land, which he gave to their fathers, and shall scatter them beyond the river, because they have made their groves, provoking the LORD to anger. And he shall give Israel up because of the sins of Jeroboam, who did sin, and who made Israel to sin. (I Kings 14:7-16)

With the agonizing reminder that he had been placed in the position of the king over ten of Israel's twelve tribes by the express prophetic word of the Lord and that he had had made a one-hundred-eighty-degree turn away from God and had led the entire nation down this perverted path with him, the prophet then declared doom upon Jeroboam, his family, and the nation as a whole. Punctuating the whole message was the death of the boy as soon as the mother crossed the threshold of their home.

Before we make any concluding summations about the

prophet-king role in the reign of Jeroboam, let's hit the back-to-the-present throttle in our time machine so I can tell you about Dr. Tunde Bakare, a friend of mine who stands in a prophetic role in the nation of Nigeria. Although he pastors a very prominent church within the country, there is no question that his mission far exceeds the local congregation. He has a television ministry in which he addresses the issues of the nation, always based on a biblical paradigm. On many occasions, he has received prophetic words that actually defined and redirected the course of the nation. With such prophetic ministry, he has won a place in the nation in which the President – who happens to be a Muslim – regularly seeks his counsel and prayer. But the story I want to relate here has to do with a prophetic declaration he once made over the United States. Long before the candidates for the 2008 election were determined, the Lord interrupted him in the middle of a Sunday morning service with the revelation that the next President of the United States would be a black man. Just as was predicted, Barak Obama – the first Afro-American to serve in that office – was sworn in as the forty-fourth President of the United States on January 20, 2009. Having campaigned on the platform, "Change," he immediately set about to bring change to the nation as he aggressive promoted the agendas of Muslims, homosexuals, and abortionists – as he, all the while, actively suppressed the voices and constitutional rights of the Christian community. Tons of rhetoric concerning climate change distracted the world as the entire climate toward godliness and rightness made a total change. Each time that our nation crossed another milestone in its moral and ethical decay during Mr. Obama's tenure in office, I would joke to Dr. Bakare that he had prophesied the man into office. It was not until actually near the end of Mr. Obama's administration that I realized that just because something is prophetically declared doesn't make it good. After all, Daniel announced the coming of the little horn (Daniel 8:9), Jesus foresaw the appearance of the abomination of desolation (Matthew 24:15), Paul predicted the rise of the son of perdition (II Thessalonians 2:3), and John foretold the manifestation of Apollyon (Revelation 9:11) – all of which prophesied the rise of the Antichrist. Therefore, just because the prophet Ahijah thrust ten of the twelve shreds of his cloak into Jeroboam's hand and proclaimed that he would rule over ten of Israel's tribes was no indication that God's favor was inherent in the prophecy.

In Jeroboam, we see an example of a king (government) who knows in his heart that the Lord is the true God but fights against that awareness "tooth and toenail." He knew that he was placed in power through the prophetic word of the Lord and he knew that he would have to go to a prophet of God when he needed an accurate prophecy concerning his son's life; however, all the while he was hell-bent on eradicating worship of that true God out of his regime and actually set a benchmark that was constantly referred to when measuring the idolatry that would permeate the rest of his nation's history. In much the same way that David became the standard for godliness, Jeroboam became the yardstick for measuring ungodliness and paganism. (I Kings 15:30, 15:34, 16:2, 16:19, 16:26, 16:31, 22:52; II Kings 3:3, 10:29, 10:31, 13:2, 13:6, 13:11, 15:9, 15:18, 15:24, 15:28, 17:2)

How Shall We Escape?

Meanwhile, back at the ranch – well, actually, back in Judah – the country was experiencing an inundation of immigrants from the northern kingdom. All the priests and Levites were flooding across the border to seek new lives in the southern kingdom under Rehoboam's rule. (II Chronicles 11:13-16) Of course, we can spiritualize this part of the story and say that they desired to be able to freely express their faith and were willing to leave everything behind in order to find that freedom of religion. But please pardon me while I suggest a much more ordinary explanation for this mass migration: they were out of work and needed jobs – they had all been fired from their positions and replaced by men who had no relationship with the God of Abraham, Isaac, and Jacob. (II Chronicles 13:9) Rather than digging in their heels and standing their ground against the tide of paganism that was engulfing their nation, they quickly sought a safer and more lucrative alternative. Rather than shining as lights in a dark land (Philippians 2:15), they opted to find a place where they could live comfortably without threat or challenge. They were, as Jesus would say, hirelings rather than true shepherds of the people. (John 10:12-13)

Although the Bible does not come across as bluntly and harshly as I have described these priests who flocked into Judah, it seems reasonable from the context that these men were nothing more than chameleons camouflaging themselves as true-blue patriots of the faith as they filled out their visa applications to enter Judah. However, within three short years, they revealed their true colors as yellow-bellied cowards when the southern kingdom turned to idolatry and they did not take a stance against the blasphemy. (II Chronicles 12:1, I Kings 14: 22-24) Interestingly enough, there is no mention of a prophet during this period of abomination against the Lord.

However, a couple years later, as the nation faced invasion by the Egyptians, Shemaiah – the same prophet who had warned Rehoboam not to go to war with the northern kingdom – reappeared and brought the leadership of the country to their knees in prayer before the invading forces brought them to their knees in conquest. (II Chronicles 12:6-7) Unfortunately, the repentance proved to be only temporary in that the summary statement concerning the reign of Rehoboam was that he did evil, because he prepared not his heart to seek the Lord. (II Chronicles 12:14) Once the Egyptians had stolen all they desired and retreated, Rehoboam made a facade of godliness by replacing the shields of gold in the temple with ones made of brass – an act which not only demonstrated his poverty compared to that of his father but also proved to be symbolic of the inferior quality of his worship for the Lord. Second Chronicles 12:15, the synopsis statement concerning Rehoboam's life and reign, tells us that there was war between Rehoboam and Jeroboam during his entire administration – a blatant rejection of the advice of the prophet Shemaiah. This verse also indicated that the seer Iddo recorded the history of Rehoboam, although we have no mention of personal interaction between the king and this prophet.

Abijah, Rehoboam's son, took the reins of the southern kingdom after his father's death and apparently established a strong relationship with the priests and turned his heart toward the Lord. In fact, according to II Chronicles 13:10, he claimed that the nation had never turned away from serving their God. Regardless of his having overlooked the paganism of his father, Abijah called upon the Lord in his confrontation with the northern kingdom and won a great victory – slaying half a million of Israel's most elite soldiers. (II Chronicles 13:17) Although there is no mention of a prophetic voice in the life of King Abijah, Iddo the prophet did chronicle his life story.

Asa, who ascended the throne after the passing of his

father, did what was good and right in the eyes of the Lord by destroying the pagan worship sites and commanding the people of Judah to seek the Lord and to follow the principles of the Mosaic law. (II Chronicles 14:2-4) One of the prophetic voices that spoke into his life was Azariah who challenged the king,

> The LORD is with you, while ye be with him; and if ye seek him, he will be found of you; but if ye forsake him, he will forsake you. Now for a long season Israel hath been without the true God, and without a teaching priest, and without law. But when they in their trouble did turn unto the LORD God of Israel, and sought him, he was found of them. And in those times there was no peace to him that went out, nor to him that came in, but great vexations were upon all the inhabitants of the countries. And nation was destroyed of nation, and city of city: for God did vex them with all adversity. Be ye strong therefore, and let not your hands be weak: for your work shall be rewarded. (II Chronicles 15:2-7)

Having also received a similar prophetic word from Azariah's father, the prophet Oded, he courageously led the nation in the ways of the Lord. However, when the northern kingdom began to encroach upon his border, Asa took all the silver and the gold from the treasures of the temple and royal family to bribe the king of Syria into league with him rather than alignment with Israel. (I Kings 15:18, II Chronicles 16:2) This alliance with a foreign power was a tragic departure from his previous stance of faith in God as portrayed in his proclamation when facing an army of a million Ethiopian warriors, "LORD, it is nothing with thee to help, whether with many, or with them that have no power: help us, O LORD our God; for we rest on thee, and in thy name we go against this multitude. O LORD, thou art our

God; let not man prevail against thee." (II Chronicles 14:11) As we would anticipate, the Lord raised up another prophetic voice to correct Asa in this time of wavering faith and confidence. Hanani confronted him with the comparison of how he had trusted the Lord when facing the Ethiopians and how he had turned to human assistance in his present situation. Reminding the king of what is probably one of the greatest promises in the Bible – that the eyes of the LORD run to and fro throughout the whole earth to show Himself strong in the behalf of those whose heart is perfect toward Him – the prophet concluded that unfortunately the king no longer qualified as one with a perfect heart and that he would, therefore, have to endure turmoil throughout the remainder of his reign. (II Chronicles 16:7-9, see also I Kings 15:14 and II Chronicles 15:17) Rather than repenting and accepting the word of the seer, Asa retaliated by throwing him into jail and initiating a persecution against "some of the people" – implying those who sided with the prophet. The tragic end of this king is that he died because he sought help from medical doctors rather than from the God who had declared that He was actively looking for opportunities to prove His strength. The irony of the whole scenario is that his disease was listed as a foot problem – not something like a heart attack, brain tumor, or lung cancer that would have been immediately considered a fatal situation.

    Paralleling Asa's reign in Judah was the rule of Baasha in Israel. First Kings 16:2-4 records an interesting proclamation given to Baasha by the prophet Jehu (Hanani's son), "Forasmuch as I exalted thee out of the dust, and made thee prince over my people Israel; and thou hast walked in the way of Jeroboam, and hast made my people Israel to sin, to provoke me to anger with their sins; Behold, I will take away the posterity of Baasha, and the posterity of his house; and will make thy house like the house of Jeroboam the son of Nebat. Him that dieth of Baasha in the city shall the dogs eat; and him that dieth of his in the fields shall the fowls of the air eat." Notice that no matter how wicked the king and the nation were during this period, the Lord still proclaimed that it was God Himself who had raised up Baasha to power and that He still spoke of Israel as His own people. Even though the prophetic word was one of doom and destruction, the ultimate message was that God was still involved in their lives regardless of their rebellion. Hanani's son Jehu continued the prophetic ministry his father had to King Asa of Judah by pronouncing these apocalyptic messages against Baasha of Israel and his administration. Though some would think that such messages of doom would be a manifestation of a judgmental God, there could also be another side to the coin in that God cared enough about the king and the nation to send messengers to them to make them aware of their evil ways and the impending consequences. Although the prophets didn't specifically offer the opportunity for repentance and redemption, we must remember that such an offer was not part of Jonah's message to the citizens of Nineveh, "Yet forty days, and Nineveh shall be overthrown" (Jonah 3:4), yet the king took the warning as an opportunity to seek the Lord's mercy and forgiveness. If God were willing to salvage a pagan city like Nineveh, certainly He would have shown mercy upon His own people.

Perhaps the lesson that we can learn from these kings is the same message communicated in Hebrews 2:3, "How shall we escape, if we neglect so great salvation; which at the first began to be spoken by the Lord, and was confirmed unto us by them that heard him."

Halting Between Opinions

Baasha was murdered by Zimri in an attempt to capture the throne. One short week later, Zimri committed suicide by burning himself to death rather than to be captured by Omri, who established himself on the throne for the following twenty-eight years. Omri's son Ahab succeeded him on the throne of Israel, introducing one of the most interesting prophet-king relationships in the nation's history. But before we discuss their interactions, we need to take just a minute to remember that Ahab married Jezebel the daughter of the king of Sidon, and adamant promoter of the worship of Baal. It was into this atmosphere of paganism that the prophet Elijah made his entry. When the prophet confronted the king over the promotion of Baal worship in the nation, he announced a devastating judgment against the country, "As the LORD God of Israel liveth, before whom I stand, there shall not be dew nor rain these years, but according to my word." (I Kings 17:1) After making the pronouncement, Elijah was directed to hide from the king on the banks of the Brook Cherith where he was supernaturally sustained until he was directed to relocate to the town of Zarephath where even more miraculous events provided for not only the prophet but also a destitute widow and her family. During the three years of draught that followed, Ahab – unaware that his governor Obadiah was a God-fearing man who had hidden a hundred prophets in caves and kept them alive with bread and water – recruited him to help find water sources to keep the military's horses alive. At this precise time, the Lord directed Elijah to show himself to the king and declare that rains were to come. (I Kings 18:1) As Elijah was on his way to find the king, his path crossed that of Obadiah who recognized the prophet and fell on his face before the prophet. When Elijah directed the governor to go back to the king and tell him that Elijah had come out of hiding, Obadiah questioned, "What have I sinned, that thou wouldest deliver thy servant into the hand of Ahab, to slay me? As the LORD thy God liveth, there is no nation or kingdom, whither my lord hath not sent to seek thee: and when they said, He is not there; he took an oath of the kingdom and nation, that they found thee not. And now thou sayest, Go, tell thy lord, Behold, Elijah is here. And it shall come to pass, as soon as I am gone from thee, that the Spirit of the LORD shall carry thee whither I know not; and so when I come and tell Ahab, and he cannot find thee, he shall slay me: but I thy servant fear the LORD from my youth." (I Kings 18:9-14) Only after a firm reassurance from the prophet, was the governor willing to go back and approach the king.

As he had promised, Elijah did make his way to the king and boldly presented himself. The king's immediate response was one of hostility – accusing the prophet that he was the one who was troubling Israel by commanding that there be no rain. Elijah's reply was that it was Ahab who was troubling the nation by leading them into the idolatry that had engendered the Lord's retribution. This confrontation led to one of the most epic scenes in the entire Bible and perhaps the history of mankind – the contest between Elijah and the prophets of Baal to call fire down from heaven.

You cannot image how tempted I am to spend the next several pages waxing eloquent in describing all that took place next – how Elijah spend much of the day taunting the prophets of Baal as they chanted, danced, and even mutilated themselves begging their god to answer their pleadings, how the prophet of God had the people pour twelve barrels of water on his sacrifice (an extravagant act of faith in that it not only drenched the kindling to the point that it would be impossible to ignite but also an excessive act of lavishness since water was more precious than gold after a three-year-long draught), and how God supernaturally answered by fire so intense that it nor only burned up all the combustible sacrifice but also consumed the very rocks that had been used to construct the altar. But I have to constrain myself for two reasons. First, this study is concerned with the interactions of the prophets of God and the kings of men – not the struggle between the prophets of God and the so-called prophets of the pagans. Second, I must hurry to get to the next story – the coming of the rains that ended the draught and tension between Elijah and Ahab during this miraculous event.

After killing all the prophets of Baal, Elijah turned to King Ahab and told him to have dinner and to head for his palace so that he could avoid the coming torrents of rain. At this point, we need to consider two different aspects of this conversation. The first would be the logistics of what is happening because it reveals something of significance about the timing of the events. The confrontation between the Elijah and the prophets of Baal took place on top of Mount Carmel, the slaying of the pagan prophets took place at the Brook Kishon (which in the Jezreel Valley at the base of Mount Carmel), and Elijah's prayer for the rains to come took place on the top of the mountain. Therefore, King Ahab was already in the valley when the prophet told him to return to his palace; however the prophet then had to climb back up the mountain, pray seven times for the clouds to appear, and then climb back down the mountain and outrun the king to his palace – all in less time than it took for the king to eat and get to his home on the level road through the valley. (I Kings 18:41-46) Unless the king held an extravagant banquet before heading home – or perhaps he delayed his journey because he was afraid to face Jezebel with the news that Elijah had proven that her god was a phony and that her prophets were all dead – we can see how quickly God answered the prophet's call for rain. With a sixty-three-word prayer, he called fire down from heaven, and with seven quick prayers, he brought on a storm that made the one on the day that Saul was crowned the first king of Israel look like a spring shower. The second thing that we can understand from the scenario of these events is that the king was apparently by Elijah's side during the whole series of events that day. First Kings 18:20 tells us that Ahab sent for all the people of Israel and gathered the prophets together on Mount Carmel. Although there is no explicit statement to the fact that he himself was present, the wording seems to indicate as much in that he gathered the prophets – a term that implies that he brought them to where he was. If this is the case, then the next verse becomes very strategic in our study, "Elijah came unto all the people, and said, How long halt ye between two opinions? if the LORD be God, follow him: but if Baal, then follow him." (I Kings 18:21) Yes, Elijah was speaking to the nation as a whole, but since the king was present with them, the message was likely directly pointed to Ahab as their leader. Ahab represents a national ruler who wavered between believing in God and serving the gods of Jezebel. Even though Ahab did exceedingly evil in the sight of the Lord I Kings 16:30, 33), he still seemed to recognize that Elijah's God was one to be feared and that Elijah was a man whose words certainly demanded serious consideration.

Chapters twenty and twenty-one of I Kings take us through several dramatic encounters between Ahab and the prophets of God. In chapter twenty, we read the story of how the king of Syria twice made plans to invade Israel and take the kings treasures, including his wives and children. In both situations, a prophet (or man of God) rose up to warn and embolden Ahab. Additionally, a son of the prophets intervened to scold him for allowing the king of Syria to live when he begged for mercy after Israel's victory. Chapter twenty-one recounts the story of how Ahab allowed Jezebel to have Naboth falsely accused and executed so that he could take the poor man's vineyard. At this point Elijah reentered the life of the king in a dramatic encounter in which he gave Ahab a prophecy that sealed his personal fate and that of his entire family:

In the place where dogs licked the blood of

48

Naboth shall dogs lick thy blood, even thine. And Ahab said to Elijah, Hast thou found me, O mine enemy? And he answered, I have found thee: because thou hast sold thyself to work evil in the sight of the LORD. Behold, I will bring evil upon thee, and will take away thy posterity, and will cut off from Ahab him that pisseth against the wall, and him that is shut up and left in Israel, And will make thine house like the house of Jeroboam the son of Nebat, and like the house of Baasha the son of Ahijah, for the provocation wherewith thou hast provoked me to anger, and made Israel to sin. And of Jezebel also spake the LORD, saying, The dogs shall eat Jezebel by the wall of Jezreel. Him that dieth of Ahab in the city the dogs shall eat; and him that dieth in the field shall the fowls of the air eat. But there was none like unto Ahab, which did sell himself to work wickedness in the sight of the LORD, whom Jezebel his wife stirred up. And he did very abominably in following idols, according to all things as did the Amorites, whom the LORD cast out before the children of Israel. (I Kings 21:19-26)

As we have already seen, Ahab was vacillating between two mindsets – even though he was vehement in his service to pagan gods, he knew that the words of God spoken through the prophet Elijah were words to be reckoned with. Therefore, upon hearing these prophetic words, he ripped his clothes, put on sackcloth, and fasted – an act of humility that God honored by delaying the judgment until the reign of his son.

We find the concluding scene of Ahab's life in the following chapter when Jehoshaphat, king of the southern kingdom, comes to visit him in the northern kingdom. Since there had been an ongoing war with Syria, Ahab invited the armies of Judah to assist him in bringing closure to the conflict. Jehoshaphat said that he would not enter into the conflict without direction from a prophet, a request that Ahab was immediately able to answer by summoning four hundred prophets. Upon surveying the congregation of prophets, Jehoshaphat realized that these were not trustworthy genuine spokesmen for God and insisted that there must be a prophet of the Lord that could be consulted. Again, Ahab did not hesitate to answer that there was a prophet of the Lord by the name of Micaiah – but then quickly added that he didn't like hearing from him because his words were never favorable. The story seems to reinforce the summation that we have already seen that Ahab was a man who tittered between two opinions – even though he was determined not to follow the words of the prophet, he was somehow aware of what Micaiah was saying about his leadership. The story leads us through a series of fascinating twists and turns, but ends with Ahab's being stuck by a random arrow that – like a guided missile – found the one vulnerable spot in the king's armor. Just as Elijah had predicted, dogs found his chariot and licked up Ahab's blood before his servants had a chance to wash away the pool. So ended the life and legacy of a king whom a prophet had given the chance to decide which was the true God and worthy to be served – the Lord or Baal.

Elijah and Elisha

Even though we have seen the demise of the king who witnessed the Lord answer the prophet by sending fire out of heaven, we are still not done with the prophet who called down those celestial flames. Soon after Ahaziah took the throne after his father's death, he had an unfortunate accident and sent messengers to the Philistine city of Ekron to enquire of Baalzebub about his fate. However, the angel of the Lord intervened and sent Elijah to the messengers with the enquiry, "Is it not because there is not a God in Israel, that ye go to enquire of Baalzebub the god of Ekron?" (II Kings 1:4) He followed up on the question with the declaration that the king would not be able to regain strength to get out of bed but would die of his injuries. Apparently accepting the prophet's words as definitive, the messengers returned to the king without furthering their journey to Philistia. When they reported the prophecy to Ahaziah, he asked them to describe the man who had given them the mandate. The fact that the prophet was a hairy man dressed in a leather girdle dispelled all doubt that the prophet was Elijah, enraging the king. He sent an officer with a delegation of fifty soldiers to bring in the prophet, but Elijah called fire out of heaven to consume the officer and his entourage. A repeat command by the king resulted in a repeat performance by the prophet. When the king sent a third delegation, the officer begged for mercy from Elijah and was spared the fiery death of the previous two arrest parties. With the encouragement from the angel of the Lord, the prophet went to Ahaziah's bedside and personally delivered the same decree – that he would soon die – that he had sent through the king's emissaries. This was the final prophetic word that Elijah spoke into the lives of the kings of his nation; however, his prophetic ministry did not cease with his miraculous accent into the heavens.

In an episode that we passed over as we were racing through the story of the prophet, we get a glimpse into the lingering impact of his ministry. In I Kings 19:15, we find a directive from God for Elijah to ordain three men as the leaders of the next generation: Hazael as king of Syria, Jehu as king of Israel, and Elisha as the prophet to take the place of Elijah after his ascension. Interestingly enough, Elijah only fulfilled one of these three commands. In the same chapter we see the story of his anointing Elisha as his successor in the role of the prophet of God, and, of course, we all remember the epic story from II Kings chapter two of how Elisha received a double portion of Elijah's anointing by catching his mantle upon his departure from Planet Earth. However, it may come as a surprise that it was Elisha – not Elijah himself – who anointed Hazael as king of Syria and prophesied that he would bring much death and suffering upon the people of Israel. (II Kings 8:7-13) Even more amazing is the fact that it was an unnamed disciple of Elisha who anointed Jehu to his position as king of Israel. (II Kings 9:1-10) Just as Paul taught Timothy that what he received from the apostle was to be advanced into further generations (II Timothy 2:2), so the prophetic anointing on Elijah was so tangibly transferable that God considered the actions two generations later to be the works of the prophet himself.

In the life of Elisha, we can see some important lessons concerning the position of authority of a true prophet in relationship to the king in political power and the interaction between the king and the prophet.

The first incident that I'd like to explore is found in the third chapter of II Kings when Jehoram king of Israel found himself facing the formidable army of Moab. Even though he was in alliance with the kings of Edom and Judah and might have had the manpower to defeat the enemy, he was constrained by the simple strategic flaw of gathering the armies into array at a place that was a seven-day journey away from a viable water source. Facing this almost certain defeat, Jehoram sent forty camels laden with gifts to Elisha and requested an audience with the prophet. Elisha's response was that he would not even consider such a meeting with the king of the northern kingdom except that he had respect for the king of the southern kingdom – no matter what gifts were offered to him. He then prophesied a miraculous supply of water without any apparent source and the resulting great victory over the Moabites.

The following chapter tells the story of Elisha and his benefactor, a wealthy Shunammite woman. When the prophet wanted to show gratitude to her for her generous hospitality, one of the options that he suggested was that he could speak to the king on her behalf (II Kings 4:13), suggesting that the prophet had access to the throne at his volition. Of course, we know the rest of the story – that the woman's need was not royal privilege but to be able to bear a son. The follow-up to this part of the narrative is that she did have the much-coveted baby within a year but that the boy died while still a young child; however, Elisha supernaturally called the lad's spirit back into his body and raised him from the dead – an event that sets the stage for a future king-prophet relationship.

But first, let's keep chronological order and look at the story of Naaman, a high-ranging officer of Syria. When the general was diagnosed with leprosy, he was understandably very disturbed and was willing to listen to anyone who could suggest a possible remedy – even one of his slaves. When his wife's maid spoke of the possibility that the prophet in Judah could cure the master, Naaman immediately asked that the king of Syria make arrangements for an emissary to visit with the king of Judah. Unfortunately the king of Israel mistook the official letter from the king of Syria as a threat and assumed that it was a trick to pick a fight. Fortunately, word of the request reached the prophet, and he volunteered to intervene by healing Naaman. In spite of how interesting the rest of the story is, we must be careful not to get sidetracked into elaborating on it since our purpose here is to focus on the interaction between the king and the prophet. So leaving behind Naaman's initial arrogance and his ultimate decision to dip seven times in the Jordan River and the eventual transfer of his leprosy to Elisha's gold-digging servant Gehazi, let's simply say that this episode in the life of Elisha reveals to us the nature of the relationship between the prophet and the king in that the prophet was there to intervene when the king needed his support.

In spite of the fact that his trusted general had been healed of leprosy in Israel, the king of Syria eventually did follow through with evil intents toward the king of the northern kingdom and sent in forces to ravage the land. By chapter six of II Kings, we find record of continuous Syrian raids on and forays into the land of Israel. Yet each one was spoiled by counterintelligence strategies on the part of the Israelite forces. When the king of Syria suspected that there was a "mole" (traitor serving as a spy for the enemy) among his inside circle, his confidant answered, "Elisha, the prophet that is in Israel, telleth the king of Israel the words that thou speakest in thy bedchamber." (II Kings 6:12) In response, the king sent a large contingency of soldiers and cavalry to arrest the prophet. The ensuing events are almost beyond description. As the troops surrounded the prophet's house, his fearful servant rushed in to tell the man of God about their impending doom. Elisha simply answered that there were more on their side than were on the side of the enemy. Excusing himself with the fact that he was a Bible student rather than a mathematics scholar, the servant insisted that he could still count well enough to see that were only two of them and hundreds of Syrian soldiers. After the prophet prayed that the servant would have his spiritual eyes opened to see into the supernatural realm, the young man came back to report that the entire mountain range was infested with angelic forces warring on behalf of the prophet and his young intern. With this assurance of supernatural reinforcements, the prophet commanded that the Syrian forces be temporarily blinded, and he led them unknowingly to the palace of the Israelite king. Then – just as he had prayed that the servant be given supernatural vision – the prophet restored the natural sight to the Syrians, and they realized that they were trapped. Even though the king desired to slaughter the forces, Elisha had another plan – feed them and send them home unharmed. This was a dramatically symbolic act in the context of what was to happen next – a massive invasion of the land and such an effective blockade of the capital that the people were starving to the point that the people turned to cannibalism with women even eating their own babies. At the height of this horrible campaign, the king of Israel decided to execute Elisha. Of course, God had another plan – one that involved the opening of the windows of heaven and supplying lavishly for the people of Israel by sending four leprous beggars to find that Syrian army had evacuated their camp leaving behind a sumptuous supply of food along with great riches. No matter how dramatic this fascinating chapter of the story may be, we must be careful not to let the exhilaration of the narrative overshadow our purpose of the study – the tension between the role of the prophet and the position of the king. We must stop to realize that within just eleven verses the king went from calling Elisha his father (II Kings 6:21) to planning his execution (II Kings 6:31).

    Now back to the Shunammite woman. When a famine threatened the land, Elisha advised her to move her business to Philistia for seven years rather than lose everything by trying to function in the downturned markets in Israel. After her return to her homeland, she needed royal approval to reclaim her property from squatters who had taken up residence on her premises. By divinely orchestrated coincidence, Elisha's servant Gehazi – who had apparently been healed of the leprosy he had contracted after his greedy episode with Naaman (otherwise, he would have never been allowed back into public life) – was serving in the king's court at that exact time. And by even more supernatural timing, the king had requested that Gehazi recite to him the miraculous experiences of his life with Elisha. With the same exact precision that He choreographs the movement of the sun, moon, and planets, the Lord directed that the Shunammite woman would walk into the throne room at the exact moment that Gehazi was recounting the story of the raising of her son from the dead! Pardon me, but again I must insist that we not get too involved with the story itself that we miss to point that we are mining for in the story – the relationship between the king and the prophet. The detail that we must not overlook here is that the king had requested that Gehazi reminisce with him about the works of Elisha – a telltale element that gives us great insight into the tension between the two offices.

The first encounter between the two men was when the king was facing the armies of Moab, and the king sent a massive gift to the prophet in order to curry his favor to prophesy over the situation. Elisha's response was that he was unmoved by the gift and only consented to assist because of the presence of the king of Judah. Of course, he prophesied a supernatural deliverance and victory for the king. Although their next interaction was only implied, it seemed clear that the prophet had gained essentially unlimited access to the king in that he offered to arrange a royal audience for the Shunammite woman if that was what she would request. Next we saw that the prophet had been taken into the king's circle of advisors because he was able to speak to the king on an apparently daily basis to supernaturally advise him of the strategies of the Syrian army. The fact that the communication was apparently two-way is revealed in the following encounter in which the prophet was advised of the dilemma in which the king found himself when the Syrian king sent Naaman to Israel to be healed of his leprosy. The incident with the blinded Syrian troops shows us the level respect in which the king held to prophet when he spoke of him as his father. Yet the story of the king's desire to execute the prophet shows us a total reversal in this attitude. But this narrative about his desire to reminisce about the prophet's life shows us again that the king held him in a place of honor and respect.

By the time of Elisha's death, both the northern and southern kingdoms had gone through a tumultuous time and had seen both peaceful and hostile changes in their rulers. Israel's reigning monarch at the time was Joash, who apparently had a deep love and respect for the prophet in that II Kings 13:14 records that he personally came to Elisha's bedside when he fell sick and wept over him, calling the prophet, "My father." The prophet's last words were directions for the king to strike the ground with his arrows and to shoot them out the window toward the east. In prophetic insight, Elisha was able to discern the level of courage and faith in the young king – a level that would ensure that he could win victories over the enemy, but not enough to totally defeat them.

Believe the Prophets and Prosper

Entering our time machine once again, let's shift to hoover mode so we can get a bird's eye view of the next several generations without having to focus on the details on individual kings and prophets.

For so it was, that the children of Israel had sinned against the LORD their God, which had brought them up out of the land of Egypt, from under the hand of Pharaoh king of Egypt, and had feared other gods, And walked in the statutes of the heathen, whom the LORD cast out from before the children of Israel, and of the kings of Israel, which they had made. And the children of Israel did secretly those things that were not right against the LORD their God, and they built them high places in all their cities, from the tower of the watchmen to the fenced city. And they set them up images and groves in every high hill, and under every green tree: And there they burnt incense in all the high places, as did the heathen whom the LORD carried away before them; and wrought wicked things to provoke the LORD to anger: For they served idols, whereof the LORD had said unto them, Ye shall not do this thing. Yet the LORD testified against Israel, and against Judah, by all the prophets, and by all the seers, saying, Turn ye from your evil ways, and keep my commandments and my statutes, according to all the law which I commanded your fathers, and which I sent to you by my servants the prophets. Notwithstanding they would not hear, but hardened their necks, like to the neck of their fathers, that did not believe in the LORD their God. And they rejected his statutes, and his covenant that he made with their fathers, and his testimonies which he testified against them; and they followed vanity, and became vain, and went after the heathen that were round about them, concerning whom the LORD had charged them, that they should not do like them. And they left all the commandments of the LORD their God, and made them molten images, even two calves, and made a grove, and worshipped all the host of heaven, and served Baal. And they caused their sons and their daughters to pass through the fire, and used divination and enchantments, and sold themselves to do evil in the sight of the LORD, to provoke him to anger. Therefore the LORD was very angry with Israel, and removed them out of his sight: there was none left but the tribe of Judah only. Also Judah kept not the commandments of the LORD their God, but walked in the statutes of Israel which they made. And the LORD rejected all the seed of Israel, and afflicted them, and delivered them into the hand of spoilers, until he had cast them out of his sight. For he rent Israel from the house of David; and they made Jeroboam the son of Nebat king: and Jeroboam drave Israel from following the LORD, and made them sin a great sin. For the children of Israel walked in all the sins of Jeroboam which he did; they departed not from them; Until the LORD removed Israel out of his sight, as he had said by all his servants the prophets. So was Israel carried away out of their own land to Assyria unto this day. (II Kings 17:7-23)

With this overview of the next generations of prophetic ministry, we see that the work of the prophets was basically to warn the people – including, of course, the leadership of kings and priest – of impending judgment due to their sinful ways and pagan practices.

However, we do see an occasional anomaly such as the ministry of the prophet Isaiah who is introduced in chapter nineteen of II Kings. The setting of the appearance of this new voice from God is during the reign of Judah's godly King Hezekiah. The Assyrian king had initiated psychological warfare against the people of Jerusalem by sending a messenger to spread intimidating propaganda among the people in telling them that they should surrender without a fight since it was obvious from the previous victories of the Assyrian army over all the surrounding countries that no army and no national deity was powerful enough to withstand their invasion. Facing such insurmountable odds, Hezekiah made the public display of humility before the Lord by rending his clothes and donning sackcloth as he retreated into the temple to seek counsel and courage. In the house of God, he found men of faith whom he could send to the prophet's house where they received the declaration of God from Isaiah, "Be not afraid of the words which thou hast heard, with which the servants of the king of Assyria have blasphemed me. Behold, I will send a blast upon him, and he shall hear a rumour, and shall return to his own land; and I will cause him to fall by the sword in his own land." (II Kings 19:6-7) The encouragement was relatively short-lived as the Assyrians did retreat temporarily but soon resumed their threats and assault, forcing the king back into the temple to cry out to the Lord that He would prove that the God of Judah – unlike the idols of the other nations that had succumbed to the

Assyrian onslaught – was a true and living God. The answer came in a more detailed message from the prophet Isaiah in which he proclaimed that the Assyrian army would be turned back the same way that they came against Judah without even shooting one arrow into the city of Jerusalem. The prophecy continued on to say that the people of Judah and Jerusalem would be planted and prosper because God had determined to defend the city and to save it for His own sake and for the sake of His servant David. (II Kings 19:20-34) That same night, one hundred eighty-five thousand soldiers mysteriously died with no apparent cause other than the Lord's vengeance.

Chapter twenty of II Kings recounts the fascinating story of Hezekiah's brush with death and miraculous recovery – again, an act of intervention by the prophet Isaiah. At the first sign of the seriousness of the king's ailment, the prophet gave him the divine message that his ailment would lead to his death. However, when Hezekiah did some serious intercession and pleaded with God to honor the fact that he had lived a godly life and served Him with a perfect heart (the principle to success that he had apparently learned from King David's testimony), the Lord sent the prophet back to the king's palace with a different message – that Hezekiah was to live an additional fifteen years. Unfortunately, two tragic things happened during those extended years – Hezekiah bore a son who would succeed him on the throne and rule as one of the nation's most wicked kings (II Kings 21:11) and Hezekiah allowed the Babylonian emissaries who came to wish him well after his recovery to tour the nation's treasury, an act that stimulated their greed and eventually led to an invasion of the country (II Kings 20:12-18). But back to the story of the interaction between the king and the prophet. Because the prophet's message was such an amazing answer to his prayers, Hezekiah found it hard to believable that it was actually true and requested that Isaiah confirm it with some sort of supernatural sign. Isaiah answered the request by causing the sundial to actually back up in time – an act that literally required the entire solar system to reverse its movement! In other words, God literally suspended the natural laws that hold the universe together for one king and one prophet!

In the lives of Hezekiah and Isaiah we see what is likely the epitome of how God intended a prophet to function in the life of a king. When a king has a heart that is pure before God and is willing to live humbly before Him, the Lord sends him a man who can move heaven and earth for the benefit of the godly leader's rule.

Another anomaly that we see as we go through Judah's historical annals is the reign of Josiah, the king who was placed on the throne at the tender age of eight years old. The summation of his rule is given in II Kings 22:2 – that he did that which was right in the sight of the Lord and walked in all the way of David his father without turning aside either to the right hand or the left. The major project that his reign is remembered for was the cleansing and repair of the temple in Jerusalem, but one significant byproduct of this project was that the book of the law (likely Deuteronomy) was discovered inside the temple during the renovations. When Josiah became aware of all the judgments that were spelled out in the divine law against his nation because of all the sins that his forefathers had led the people into, King Josiah went into anguish and mourning and commanded that the priests intercede before God in hope that there might be a way out for him and his people. Through a series of connections, the priests eventually found Huldah the prophetess who had the word of God for the king – that the judgments would certainly be meted out but that He would delay the consequences until after the king's death because God honored the facts that Josiah's heart was tender and that he was willing to humble himself before the Lord. Second Kings chapter twenty-three follows up on the story of Josiah by saying that he stood before all the people to make a covenant to serve the Lord, that he led the people in renewing their lives to God, and that he destroyed the sacrileges that polluted the nation dating as far back as the time of King Solomon. In the process, King Josiah fulfilled the prophecy spoken by the man of God who appeared before King Jeroboam when he set up the first pagan altar in Bethel. The record of Josiah's life confirms that there was no other king before or after him who turned to the Lord with all his heart, soul, and might according to all the law of Moses as he did (II Kings 23:25) and that he observed the Passover in a manner that had not been seen since the days of Samuel (II Chronicles 35:18). However, the interesting thing about this great reformer is that we see no further record of a prophetic influence in his life after this one dramatic word from Hulda – proof that one true prophetic intervention is all that is needed to set the course of history and destiny.

Another remarkable prophetic connection in the lineage of the kings of Judah was the intervention of Azariah son of Obed in the life of King Asa. Although Azariah is never spoken of as a prophet per se, II Chronicles chapter fifteen describes an incident in which the Spirit of God came upon him and he went out to meet Asa with the message, "The Lord will be with you as long as you are with Him. If you seek Him, He will be found of you; however, if you forsake Him, He will forsake you." Azariah went on to say that it had been a very long time since Judah had truly served the Lord or even had a priesthood that taught or executed the Word of the Lord. He encouraged the king to be strong so that his works would be rewarded. Asa's response was that he took the prophecies of Azariah and those of his father Oded to heart and cleansed the country of the all its idolatrous relics, held a great covenant renewal service for the people, and restored all the treasures to the temple. God rewarded his dedication by granting him the next thirty-five-years of his reign as an unprecedented period of peace uninterrupted by war. Unfortunately, the king's trust in and dependence upon the Lord faltered when King Baasha of

Israel attacked. Asa used the temple treasury to hire the armies of Syria as mercenaries to defend his nation. At this point, God sent the seer Hanani to warn the king of his foolishness. Extending probably the most powerful promise ever recorded in the holy scripture – that God was actively looking for a chance to prove His strength by intervening on behalf of those whose hearts are perfect before Him (II Chronicles 16:9) – the seer then immediately pointed toward the king and declared that he no longer qualified (II Chronicles 15:17). Because of this prophetic reprimand, the seer wound up in jail. The prophetic word also led to the king's final demise – as we have seen earlier in our study – from a disease that would normally not be considered fatal.

In II Chronicles chapter twenty, we find the familiar story of King Jehoshaphat's predicament when he found himself facing overwhelming odds against the combined forces of the Moabites, the Ammonites, and the men of Mount Seir. We so often remember the "punch line" of the story in which the king commanded the praisers to go out first before the warriors. However, the meat of the story is the part that leads up to this unusual decision. When the king first found himself in this impossible situation, he determined to seek the Lord and entered into a fast. Having called the nation to intercession, he stood before the new court of the temple and cried out with a prayer based on the proposition that Solomon had prayed when he dedicated the sanctuary – that God would intervene for the nation when the people humbled themselves and called upon Him for help in times of trouble. At that point Jahaziel, who interestingly enough was never given the official title of a prophet, came by the Spirit with a word for the king and nation – that the people should not fear or be dismayed because God Himself was going to fight their battle for them. (II Chronicles 20:14-17) When Jehoshaphat addressed the people the following morning, he commanded them to believe the Lord so that they would be established and to believe His prophets so that they would prosper. (II Chronicles 20:20) It was only after this prophetic intervention that the king took courage to implement the unusual plan of sending an unarmed choir and orchestra ahead of the military. Had it not been for the king's contrite heart followed by the visit of Jahaziel, there is no way to guess how this confrontation would have played out. Perhaps we can get a glimpse of how differently things could have turned out by pushing the gas pedal on our time machine a racing forward to the reign of King Amaziah.

Second Chronicles chapter twenty-eight records a story filled with enigmatic twists and turns as it recounts the life of King Amaziah's vacillations in his faith. Facing battle against the inhabitants of Edom and Mount Seir, he hired soldiers from the northern kingdom to reinforce his troops; however, just before they engaged in battle, a man of God appeared with the message that God would not bless the union of the two nations since Israel was in a backslidden state. Amaziah questioned what he should do because he had already paid the men of Israel a large nonrefundable sum, but the prophet's reassurance that God could return to him far more than he had lost convinced the king to follow the prophetic mandate. Unfortunately, the story takes a downward turn at this point in that the offended mercenaries attacked several cities in Judah, killing three thousand innocent victims and taking a great spoil. An even more inexplicable twist comes when the king successfully defeats the Edomites and men of Seir but decides to worship the gods of his vanquished foes rather than the God who had guaranteed his victory in the battle. The Lord gave him one more chance by sending another prophet into his life, but Amaziah refused to heed his counsel, asking what right he had to advise the king and threatening to kill the prophet. The next sidewinder in the tale is that Amaziah then challenged the king of Israel to a battle that resulted in a devastating loss for Judah, the raiding of the king's personal treasury and that of the temple, and an eventual assassination plot against Amaziah. A story that began with the prophetic promise of prosperity ended with the loss of all that had been accumulated over years of careful business management – all because the king had a heart of his own rather than a willingness to heed the words of the messengers that God sent into his life.

Though Jeremiah is one of the major prophets in the Bible, he makes only a cameo appearance in the historical section of the Old Testament when he predicted the rise of the Babylonian empire and the seventy years of captivity that the people of Israel would be doomed to serve under their rule – all followed by a supernatural revelation that would be given to Cyrus in order for them to be free to go back to Palestine to rebuilt their nation and temple. (II Chronicles 36:21-22) Verse sixteen of this same chapter gives us a synopsis of how Jeremiah and his fellow prophets fared in the Judean kingdom, "They mocked the messengers of God, and despised his words, and misused his prophets, until the wrath of the LORD arose against his people, till there was no remedy." According to the extra-biblical rabbinic records, Jehoiakim (one of the kings who ruled during this time period) lived in incest with his mother and practiced human sacrifice. During his reign, he persecuted Jeremiah and ordered the execution of the prophet Uriah son of Shemaiah, becoming the only Judean king to murder a prophet. However, we can also see the story in II Chronicles chapter twenty-four of a time when the people of Judah had become resistant to the words of the prophets and refused to hear what they had to say. At this point, Zechariah the son of Jehoiada the priest stood up to speak prophetically to the people even though he was from the priestly order rather than the bands of the the prophets. Convicted in their hearts, the people conspired to stone Zechariah to death – which they did with the consent of the king.

Do It Anyway

At this point in our study, I feel a lot like the author of the book of Hebrews who after giving a survey of some of the great heroes of faith in the Old Testament simply throws his hands in the air and exclaims, "What shall I more say? Time would fail me to tell of Gideon, Barak, Samson, Jephthah, David, Samuel, and all the other prophets." Certainly, we could continue this study for chapter after chapter; however, it seems that we have presented enough case studies to be able to take some time to begin to analyze the evidence and draw some conclusions.

The first king that we considered was Saul in whom we saw an example of the king who worked in opposition to the prophet. Even though he defied the prophet, there was still an awareness in his heart that Samuel's words were genuine messages from God – otherwise, he would have never asked the witch of Endor to conjure up the dead prophet's spirit for one last word of counsel. (I Samuel 28:7-25). In David, we saw the example of a man who truly loved God and was actually reported as being a man after God's own heart. (Acts 13:22) David, the man who served the Lord with a perfect heart (I Kings 11:4, 15:3; Psalm 101:2), found himself involved in external actions that did not match up with his internal attitude – and would have covered them up with the likely result of having his heart turned away from the God he so desperately loved (Psalm 51:10) had it not been for the intervention of the prophet Nathan. Solomon reveals an unusual characteristic in that he had a clear enough relationship with God that he didn't require prophetic intervention during his reign. The division of the kingdoms that took place after the death of King Solomon energized a whole new wave of the voice of the prophets as Jeroboam received an advance notice of all that was to happen from the prophet Ahijah. Unfortunately, his personal strategy to keep his subjects loyal to him led him to introduce paganism in the northern kingdom – an error which invoked the condemnation of the man of God whom the king recognized as a legitimate spokesman of the Lord even though he did not submit himself to the prophetic correction. In Jeroboam, we saw an example of king who knew in his heart that the Lord is the true God but fought against that awareness "tooth and toenail." Rehoboam heard the words of the prophets who spoke into his life but summarily rejected them because he did not prepare his heart to seek the Lord. Asa was an interesting subject in that he was actually described as having a perfect heart before God – a quality attributed to no other king other than David himself. During the time that his heart was totally in tune with the Lord, he heard and heeded the words of the prophets that spoke into his life. Unfortunately, when the greatest possible prophetic word that was ever given to any human being was offered to him, he was disqualified because his heart was no longer stayed on the Lord. In Baasha of the northern kingdom, we saw an excellent example of a king whom God exalted to his position but simply neglected the fact that God was his source and, therefore, failed tragically. After a couple turnovers on the throne, Ahab established himself in Israel and – along with his Phoenician wife Jezebel – promoted paganism in the northern kingdom. His reign exemplified the perplexing dichotomy that an exist in a human soul when one knows and actually acknowledges the truth but is too much under the influence of others to resist peer pressure – no matter how harmful the consequences might be. In Ahaziah, we see an example of a king who deliberately made a decision to seek the advice of false prophets when the counsel of a true prophet of God was readily available. In spite of the many positive encounters between King Jehoram and the prophet Elisha, this Israelite king swore at one point that he was determined to kill the prophet because of the troubles that had befallen his people. His story is an example of the volatile nature of a ruler under pressure when he feels that he has to find a subject upon whom to shift the blame – even if the only convenient subject he can find is his ally. The story of Amaziah again reminds us of the fickle nature of men in public office who can make one-eighty turns when the political pressure becomes too great – even when they know the prophetic word that has been declared over their administrations. Joash, Hezekiah, Jehoshaphat, and Josiah – along with most of the reign of Asa – are the few bright spots in our study of the historical records where we see kings who had sensitive hearts for the Lord and respectful relationships with His prophets.

So what does this survey of the kings of Israel and Judah seem to say to us? Perhaps the most important lesson we can learn is that even though God will not do anything in His universe unless He first reveals it through His prophets (Amos 3:7), the role of the prophets is simply that of being messengers of those divine secrets. It is not the prophet's responsibility to change the course of history or destiny – that power, of course lies ultimately in the hand of the Lord Himself, but for the most part He has relegated it into the hands of the political leaders of the nations during this present dispensation of time. As we learned in II Kings 17:13, the prophets and seers are set in place to testify to the national leaders and warn them of the consequences of their actions and decisions. It is not the responsibility of the prophet to make or enforce policy – only to advise and counsel those whose role it is to actually legislate public procedure. In Proverbs 21:1, Solomon – who served in the office of both king and prophet – declared that the king's heart is in the hand of the Lord. Just as He directs the rivers of water, the Lord – not the prophet – can turn the king's heart according to His will. With that being said, it would be good for all those who stand in any prophetic position to remember the words of a little poem that was assumedly composed by Mother Teresa because it was found written on the wall in her home for children in Calcutta.

> People are often unreasonable, irrational, and self-centered. Forgive them anyway.
> If you are kind, people may accuse you of selfish, ulterior motives. Be kind anyway.
> If you are successful, you will win some unfaithful friends and some genuine enemies. Succeed anyway.
> If you are honest and sincere people may deceive you. Be honest and sincere anyway.
> What you spend years creating, others could destroy overnight. Create anyway.
> If you find serenity and happiness, some may be jealous. Be happy anyway.
> The good you do today, will often be forgotten. Do good anyway.
> Give the best you have, and it will never be enough. Give your best anyway.
> In the final analysis, it is between you and God. It was never between you and them anyway.

Jeremiah learned this lesson the hard way when he found himself beaten and imprisoned for his prophecies. In the face of these persecutions, he declared that he would never speak in the name of the Lord again, but found that he could not restrain himself because the word of the Lord was like a fire raging inside his very bones. (Jeremiah 20:9)

A second lesson that we can see illustrated in the lives of these Old Testament prophets has to do with the ability to see the invisible. Of course, the most obvious examples of this principle were Elisha's prayer that his servant's eyes be opened so that he could see the host of angelic warriors protecting them (II Kings 6:17) and blind Ahijah's discerning Jeroboam's wife (I Kings 14:5), but we see this principle in operation time and again – such as when Samuel knew about Saul's missing donkeys without having been told (I Samuel 9:20) and when Elisha knew all the secrets that were whispered in the Syrian king's bedchamber (II Kings 6:12). In the ministry of the present-day prophetic voices to the nations, this ability to see the unseen is called faith (Hebrews 11:1, 11:7), and it has to do with the ability to discern and distinguish between what situations are of simply temporary significance and which conditions carry eternal consequences (II Corinthians 4:18). The prophetic voices of today must, therefore, be able to realize which issues deserve their attention and then have the unwavering faith to address them with the boldness and courage necessary to be heard and with the eloquence and finesse to be listened to.

New Testament Kings, Priests, and Prophets

Having concluded the previous chapter with a couple statements about present-day prophetic voices, it is time to address a question that has certainly been in the minds of many of my readers, "But you've been talking about Old Testament, and we live in the New Testament – what's the relationship?" After all, I did start out explaining the different dispensations and how God as dealt with mankind differently in each changing dispensation; therefore, we do need to take a serious look at the New Testament to see if there has been a significant change in the roles of prophets and kings after the cross.

The first issue that we must consider is that Jesus came to establish the kingdom of God or heaven – not the kingdom of Israel or Judah – on earth. (Matthew 4:17, 4:23, 5:3, 5:10, 5:19, 5:20, 6:10, 6:13, 6:33, 7:21, 8:11, 8:12, 9:35, 10:7, 11:11, 11:12, 12:28, 13:11, 13:19, 13:2, 13:31, 13:33, 13:38, 13:41, 13:43, 13:44, 13:45, 13:47, 13:52, 16:19, 16:28, 18:1, 18:3, 18:4, 18:23, 19:12, 19:14, 19:23, 19:24, 20:1, 20:21, 21:31, 21:43, 22:2, 23:13, 24:14, 25:1, 25:14, 25:34, 26:29; Mark 1:14, 1:15, 4:11, 4:26, 4:30, 9:1, 9:47, 10:14, 10:15, 10:23, 10:24, 10:25, 11:10, 12:34, 14:25, 15:43; Luke 4:43, 6:20, 7:28, 8:1, 8:10, 9:2, 9:11, 9:27, 9:60, 9:62, 10:9, 10:11, 11:2, 11:20, 12:31, 12:32, 13:18, 13:20, 13:28, 13:29, 14:15, 16:16, 17:20, 17:21, 18:16, 18:17, 18:24, 18:25, 18:29, 19:11, 21:31, 22:16, 22:18, 22:29, 22:30, 23:42, 23:51; John 3:3, 3:5) In spite of the fact that His teachings were continually peppered with this message, it was a concept that even His closest disciples still couldn't grasp in that after the resurrection they were still looking for Jesus to restore the kingdom of Israel (Acts 1:6) even though He was still speaking to them about the heavenly kingdom (Acts 1:3). Additionally, it was a message that was misinterpreted by the populace in general to the point that it became a major issue at His trial with His being accused of posing as the king of the Jews. (Matthew 27:11, 27:29, 27:37, 27:42; Mark 15:2, 15:9, 15:12, 15:18, 15:26, 15:32; Luke 23:2, 23:3, 23:37, 23:38; John 18:33, 18:37, 18:39, 19:3, 19:12, 19:14, 19:15, 19:19, 19:21) When Pilate asked Jesus if He were indeed a king, Jesus responded with the answer that yes, He was a king; but no, His kingdom was not an earthly one. He went on to explain that things would be very different if He had actually come to establish an earthly kingdom in that His disciples would actively engage in physical warfare to defend Him and establish His rule. (John 18:36) But before we leave that thought, we must recall the prayer that He had prayed just the evening before over these disciples that He now spoke of as being willing to fight for a physical kingdom, "I pray not that thou shouldest take them out of the world, but that thou shouldest keep them from the evil. They are not of the world, even as I am not of the world." (John 17:15-16) No, His disciples (and, therefore, His kingdom) were not of the present world; but yes, His disciples (and, therefore, His kingdom) were to be present, active, and influential in the present world. In essence, His followers are to wage warfare in the present world since they are to remain in the present world – all the while they are to also build the kingdom that is not of this world. They are actually called to do battle on two fronts – the visible and the invisible. But before we can really understand the nature of these two battlefronts, there are a couple other New Testament principles that we must consider.

First of all, we must understand that in this new dispensation the believers are now the kings and priests of the kingdom order. (I Peter 2:9; Revelation 1:6, 5:10) In the Old Testament these two positions were distinctly separated and were actually mutually exclusive. There are two examples in which kings were severely judged for trying to cross over into the role of the priest. Saul was confronted by Samuel when he offered a sacrifice in a ceremony that should have officiated over by the priest (I Samuel 13:9), and Azariah along with a company of eighty priests withstood King Uzziah when his "heart was lifted up to his destruction" and he entered the temple to burn incense. (II Chronicles 26:16-20) Of course, it can be argued that Saul's demise came because of his rebellion and stubbornness (I Samuel 15:23) and that Uzziah's leprosery came upon him because of his pride (II Chronicles 26:16); however, we must not overlook the fact that both these kings' journeys to their Waterloos took them through an attempt to usurp the power of the office of the priest.

In the New Testament, these two offices are merged and all believers are ordained to this new royal priestly role. The resulting paradigm shift is that now the ministry that the prophets of the Old Testament were called into in relationship to the physical leaders (kings and priests) in Israel and Judah is now directed to the general body of believers. But before we can get a full grasp of how this principle works, we have to understand the second paradigm shift that has occurred in the present dispensation – the addition of a second prophetic role in the Body of Christ. In the Old Testament, the office of the prophet was an exclusive office that could be filled by only a few select individuals in each generation. However, as early as the exodus from Egypt, Moses declared that it would be desirable for all the people of God to become prophets (Numbers 11:29) – a blessing that was fulfilled in the New Testament through the impartation of the gift of prophecy (I Corinthians 14:1, 14:24, 14:31, 14:39). This prophetic gift is different from the office of a prophet in that it is a supernatural ability available to any believer so that he can speak edification (strengthening), exhortation (encouragement), and comfort (consolation) into the lives of other members of the Body of Christ. (I Corinthians 14:3) In fact, the point could be argued that one of the most significant functions within the Body of Christ is to strengthen and encourage one another. (Romans 14:19, 15:2; I Corinthians 8:1, 14:5, 14:12, 14:26; II Corinthians 10:8, 12:19, 13:10; Ephesians 4:12, 4:16, 4:29; I Thessalonians 5:11; I Timothy 1:4) Significantly, we are individually admonished to keep ourselves personally strengthened and encouraged (I Corinthians 14:4, Ephesians 5:19; Jude 1:20) and then to make that encouragement contagious to all those around us (I Corinthians 12:7, 14:4; Colossians 3:16). Why? Simply because we all need that strength to stand against the diabolical kingdom of this present world. (II Corinthians 4:4; Ephesians 6:10-12) Therefore, in the same way that the prophets of the Old Testament were to speak into the lives of the physical leaders of Israel and Judah to direct them in their confrontations with the enemy forces and paganism of their day, we all become prophets to all the other members of the Body of Christ as they serve in their roles as kings and priests who are resisting the spiritual forces in our present world. This is the invisible dimension of our mission in the present age. Yes, we can see the visible church and other Christian ministries such as evangelistic and humanitarian aid organizations in action as they serve the needy and change lives, but this is only a glimpse of what is happening; it is far from the total picture. As with Elijah, this is only the cloud the size of a man's hand foreshadowing the abundance of rain that is pouring out in the unseen realms as the prophets speak into the lives of the kings in the spiritual dimension. The Apostle Paul acknowledged this off-the-radar hurricane that is brewing behind the scenes in Romans 8:18-22 when he wrote that the whole creation is in travail and that it groans in earnest expectation of the time when the full manifestation of the dominion of the sons of God will be made manifest. The truth is that we have more powerful weapons (II Corinthians 10:3-5) and greater resources (I Corinthians 2:9-10) available to us than any of our enemies have ever imagined; all we need to do is to realize what we actually have (Ephesians 1:16-23);

therefore, we must encourage and strengthen one another to find and exercise our authority in this present age.

When Paul described the spiritual armor that God has provided for us when we are preparing to exert our authority against the forces of evil in the present age, he concluded the section with the command to pray always with all prayer and supplication in the Spirit while watching with all perseverance and supplication for all saints. (Ephesians 6:18) He also directed us that our supplications, prayers, intercessions, and thanksgiving should cover all men – especially for the kings and those who are in authority. (I Timothy 2:1-2) Although it is obvious that he is expecting that we would pray for the public leaders, it is also likely that these prayers are to include the spiritual kings and priests in the Body of Christ. Such prayers for the physical kings as well as the spiritual kings will indeed avail much. (James 5:16) I can personally testify to having seen how prayer changed the entire of Nepal. When I was first introduced to the country in 1986, the government officially forbade the practice of Christianity in the country. Many Christians – including personal acquaints of mine – were imprisoned, tortured, ostracized, and abused because they dared to believe in Jesus. Since the nation was one of the few remaining countries in the world under the rule of a king, I felt it especially appropriated to pray as Paul had commanded Timothy for the king and to claim Solomon's words that the king's heart was in the hand of the Lord to turn at His wills. For the next four years, I prayed daily that the king would be moved to grant religious freedom in the country and allow Christians the freedom to worship and share their faith publicly. To the amazement of the whole world, the king granted a new constitution that guaranteed freedom of religion and opened the doors of the country for the spreading of the gospel – leading to one of the greatest moves toward God in modern history.

But the New Testament also insists that the role of the prophet as the voice to the visible kingdoms of the world is still a valid office. (Matthew 10:41, 11:9, 21:26; Mark 6:4; Luke 4:24, 7:16, 7:26, 7:28, 13:33, 20:6; John 4:19, 4:44, 6:14, 7:40, 9:17; I Corinthians 12:28, 12:29, 14:29, 14:32; Ephesians 2:20, 3:5, 4:11; James 5:10; Revelation 10:7, 11:10, 11:18, 16:6, 18:20, 18:24, 22:6, 22:9) It is here that we see the visible battlefront in which the prophet of God speaks to the physical political and religious kingdoms just as the Old Testament prophets addressed the kings, priests, and people of the physical nations of their time. Unfortunately, if we survey the New Testament references to the role of the prophets, we find an uncomfortable number of references to the rejection of their messages and to their martyrdom – reminiscent of the lack of heed given to the most of the Old Testament men of God. However, I don't want to suggest that prophetic voices be silenced simply because we realize that many will turn a deaf ear and that others will respond violently to the message. Quite the contrary – we must shine our lights even more brightly – realizing the darkness in the world we are called to illuminate. (Romans 13:12; II Corinthians 4:6; Ephesians 5:8, 5:11, 6:12; Philippians 2:15; Colossians 1:13; I Thessalonians 5:4, 5:5; I Peter 2:9; II Peter 1:19; I John 2:8)

When prophets dare to speak out, the Lord does miraculous things. In 1954, the little-known American evangelist Tommy Hicks was called to Argentina to fulfill the crusade commitment that another minister had left open. His suggestion to the local church committee to rent a twenty-five-thousand-seat stadium and to advertise the meetings on the radio seemed absolutely absurd. However, no one could dissuade Bro. Hicks, and he decided to make an even more daring step – to visit the Argentine dictator Juan Peron. At the presidential palace, an armed guard interrogated Bro. Hicks, who explained his whole plan to hold a salvation-healing campaign in the city. When the guard questioned the evangelist as to whether God actually healed people, Bro. Hicks insisted that He did – prompting the guard to request prayer. When he was instantly freed from pain and sickness, the guard immediately offered, "Come back tomorrow and I'll get you in to see the President." Tommy Hicks returned the next day and was soon ushered into the presence of this feared leader. He quickly explained that he wanted to conduct a salvation-healing campaign in a large stadium, with press and radio coverage. President Peron – suffering from a persistent and disfiguring skin disease that had become so noticeable that he no longer allowed photographs – asked Tommy Hicks if Jesus could heal him. As they clasped hands, the power of God immediately flowed into Peron's body and his skin became as clear as a baby's! Needless to say, Peron gave Tommy everything he requested. Within days, the crusade grounds were packed beyond capacity and the meeting had to be moved to a venue that would seat more than a hundred thousand people. During the next two months, over three million people attended the meetings and over three hundred thousand salvations and a massive number of outstanding healings were recorded.

Another significant story of a prophetic voice that echoed throughout an entire nation comes from the life of Dr. Lester Sumrall. When the Lord spoke to him to go to the Philippines to raise up a ministry there, He promised, "I will do more for you there than I have done for you anywhere else in your ministry." Knowing that there had never been any major Protestant revival in the Philippines in the history of the country and that there were very few Christians in the city, Bro. Sumrall went to Manila with great anticipation of what God was going to do. For the first several months, there was only a handful of people in his church. About the time that the congregation had grown to around fifty people, the Lord began impressing Bro. Sumrall that he was to build a barn to hold the coming harvest; so, he started building a church that would seat twenty-five hundred people. He reasoned that he needed a building of at least that size since he had left a church in the US with over a thousand adults and a thousand children in the

Sunday school each week. Everybody begged him not to build such a large a facility. His denomination thought that he would make them the laughingstock of the entire world – building a church to seat over two thousand when he only had fifty members. Protestant missionaries and prominent church leaders came to Manila to stop him because they were afraid he would take their members to fill his church. But he refused to be swayed by their arguments because he knew that God would bring a revival such as the Philippines had never seen.

One night as they were getting ready for bed, Bro. Sumrall and his wife listened to the evening news. Suddenly bloodcurdling screaming and horrifying howls come across the airwaves. The news feature was the story of a young girl incarcerated in the Bilibid Prison in Manila who had been mysteriously bitten by unseen teeth. Medical doctors and prison wardens observed as tooth marks and blood mysteriously appeared on her body. From his missionary experience, Bro. Sumrall recognized that this was demonic power tormenting her; so, he got out of bed and lay on the floor praying and travailing, asking God to send somebody to deliver the victimized girl from the demon power. But the Lord answered him, "If you don't do it, the girl will die. You are the only one in this city who knows how to cast the devil out of her." At that point, Bro. Sumrall had no way of knowing that this girl's deliverance would be the key that would open up his ministry in the Philippines and actually around the world.

He spent that night in prayer and fasting. The next morning, he called the contractor who was building the church. Since the contractor was a personal friend of the mayor, he was able to get Bro. Sumrall into the mayor's office where Bro. Sumrall asked for permission to go into the prison to pray for the girl. The story of the girl's torment had already hit the international news, and the city had sent out appeals for church leaders, psychiatrists, or somebody to come and help her – but no one was able to deliver her.

Bro. Sumrall went to pray for her, but he did not get a total victory the first day; so he went back again the second and third days. After three days of fasting and prayer, he spoke to the spirit and it left. Not only was the girl set free, but a remarkable thing happened in the city. When Bro. Sumrall was ushered back into the mayor's office with the good news that the girl had been freed, the mayor was so pleased that he asked what Bro. Sumrall wanted in return. His request was for permission to have large open-air revival meetings every night on the main plaza of the city. Within a six-week period, one hundred fifty thousand people were converted to Christ. When construction of the church was completed and the dedication service was held, the church was so jammed that most of the crowd could not get inside.

Remember the torrential rain that came upon Samuel's plea and the drenching storm that followed Elijah's intersession? Well, the modern-day prophets have an even greater promise – that of the unprecedented outpouring of spiritual rain as the Holy Spirit is to be poured out upon all the nations under their prophetic voice. (Jeremiah 5:24; Hosea 6:3; Joel 2:23, 2:28; Zechariah 10:1; Acts 2:17-18; James 5:7) In the stories of Tommy Hicks and Lester Sumrall, we see what are likely just the first little sprinkles of the prophetic move of God that is yet to come.

The Making of a Christian Nation

Now that we have comfortably scanned several millennia in our time machine, let's bring it to rest again in modern times so I can share another personal experience. I had the privilege of visiting the African nation of Zambia during the time that it was rewriting its constitution. One of the issues on the table was the question as to whether the constitution should declare the country to be a Christian nation. Although several countries recognize an official state church, Zambia was the only nation in the world whose constitution formally declared the country a Christian nation; but now with the rewriting of the constitution, there was a strong move afoot to list the country as a secular nation. Since my host in the country was a delegate on the committee to word the clause in the new constitution that would either uphold the nation's previous status or revise it, I was asked to give my input. In fact, I was actually asked to give my feelings during a live national television interview, and I followed up by giving a full message on the topic during the Sunday morning service at his church. Of course, I was cautious to explain that – as a foreigner – I was not there to get involved in politics and told the story of my experience when I was accosted by a very inebriated gentleman on a train in India. This incident happened during a time when the internal unrest that eventually led to Indira Gandhi's assassination by her own trusted bodyguard was already brewing, and the drunken man insisted that I tell him if I felt that her policies were fair or not. No matter how boisterous or violent the man became, I refused to commit myself – remarking only that as an outsider I only knew part of the story. I confessed that it seemed that she was a good leader but that I couldn't comment more because there was probably a lot that I didn't know about her. However, I felt that I could say a little more in the case of the Zambian constitution question because I could answer it from the Bible rather than contemporary politics or current events.

The Bible has a lot to say about government, and it actually determined the theocratic government of the Old Testament nation of Israel. Israel's government was originally a God-ordained leadership through prophets, priests, and judges. As we have already discussed in the opening section of this book, it was only when the people insisted that they have a king like the other nations that a secular government was put into place. From the very first notion of the institution of a secular government, the Lord declared to the people that the end result would be trouble. He even went so far as to declare that the people of Israel were literally rejecting Him in setting up a secular government. In this, are we to interpret that secular governments are wrong, sinful, and ungodly? No. In fact, the Bible has much to say about the secular governments of the world. Paul's classic teaching on the role of secular government is found in Romans 13:1-14.

> Let every soul be subject unto the higher powers. For there is no power but of God: the powers that be are ordained of God. Whosoever therefore resisteth the power, resisteth the ordinance of God: and they that resist shall receive to themselves damnation. For rulers are not a terror to good works, but to the evil. Wilt thou then not be afraid of the power? do that which is good, and thou shalt have praise of the same: For he is the minister of God to thee for good. But if thou do that which is evil, be afraid; for he beareth not the sword in vain: for he is the minister of God, a revenger to execute wrath upon him that doeth evil. Wherefore ye must needs be subject, not only for wrath, but also for conscience sake. For for this cause pay ye tribute also:

for they are God's ministers, attending continually upon this very thing. Render therefore to all their dues: tribute to whom tribute is due; custom to whom custom; fear to whom fear; honour to whom honour. Owe no man any thing, but to love one another: for he that loveth another hath fulfilled the law. For this, Thou shalt not commit adultery, Thou shalt not kill, Thou shalt not steal, Thou shalt not bear false witness, Thou shalt not covet; and if there be any other commandment, it is briefly comprehended in this saying, namely, Thou shalt love thy neighbour as thyself. Love worketh no ill to his neighbour: therefore love is the fulfilling of the law. And that, knowing the time, that now it is high time to awake out of sleep: for now is our salvation nearer than when we believed. The night is far spent, the day is at hand: let us therefore cast off the works of darkness, and let us put on the armour of light. Let us walk honestly, as in the day; not in rioting and drunkenness, not in chambering and wantonness, not in strife and envying. But put ye on the Lord Jesus Christ, and make not provision for the flesh, to fulfil the lusts thereof.

In this passage, Paul makes it explicitly clear that we are to live in total respect for and submission to the civil authorities – actually recognizing them as ministers of God. We may well wonder how we can possibly view the men and women in the halls of power as ministers of God. The first thing that we must remember at this point is that just because someone is a minster of God does not make him righteous, honest, or smart. The Bible is full of examples: Eli's sons took sexual advantage of the women who came to worship at the tabernacle of God (I Samuel 2:22), King Saul tried to kill innocent David (I Samuel 18:11), the scribes and Pharisees robbed the widows of what little they owned (Matthew 23:14), the priest and the Levite left the poor victim on the side of the road to Jericho to die (Luke 10:31-32), Jesus described His disciple Judas as actually being a devil (John 6:70), and the list goes on and on. Yet, we are to show respect to those in position by acknowledging that God has placed them there in spite of their faults. (I Samuel 26:11) This is not to say that God approves of their wickedness or that we are to sit complacently by and allow evil to proliferate. The Bible is full of examples of God's personal intervention to remove evil rulers and of His using godly men as His instruments to confront them. God personally cast down Nebuchadnezzar (Daniel 4:30-33) and Herod (Acts 12:21-23) but used human channels to bring down Jezebel (II Kings 9:30-33), Eglon (Judges 3:15-22), and many more. The prophet Hosea declared that the authorities that had been put in place were not of God (verse 8:4), and Daniel confirmed that it was totally in the power and sovereignty of God to remove and establish earthly rulers (verse 2:21). The Apostle Peter helped us understand the tension between honoring and obeying the authorities and judging their error. He wrote that we must submit ourselves to every ordinance of man, stating that it is the will of God. He then explained that through doing so we can put to silence the ignorance of foolish men in that we do not use our liberty in Christ as a disguise for our own evil intensions. (I Peter 2:13-15) However, Peter was also the one who stood before the Sanhedrin and declared, "We ought to obey God rather than men." (Acts 5:29) In essence, Peter advocated that we make every effort to live in submission to the government and its policies because the root cause behind most disobedience is evil intent in our own hearts; however, we have an obligation to withstand the government policies if they are in direct contradiction to the laws of God and if we are living in submission to those divine laws ourselves. At this point, we are called upon to make some serious introspection before we can object to the governmental authority over us. If our own actions are not motivated by honesty, integrity, and generosity, we are not in the position to question or condemn the lack of honesty, integrity, and generosity of those in position above us. However, when we are certain that our own motives and actions are pure and godly, we have a moral responsibility to bring the government into accountability. Before we examine the ways we can do so, let's go back to the life of the Apostle Paul and see what relationship he had with the government of his time. When he was arrested and threatened with beating, he took advantage of every right and privilege he had as a Roman citizen. (Acts 22:25) When there was a conspiracy against his life, Paul used his status under the Roman legal system for his protection. (Acts 23:17) When he realized that extradition to Jerusalem would seal his doom, the apostle exercised his legal right of appeal to ensure that he not fall into the deathtrap set for him by the Jewish officials. (Acts 25:11) So, we see that Paul did not see himself as an enemy of the state or the state as his adversary. In fact, even when the government had imprisoned him and was ready to execute him, Paul seemed to say that even their act of killing him would be a fulfillment of God's will and, therefore, a blessing to him. (Philippians 1:21) He even served as a divine advisor to the government on at least one occasion (Acts 27:9-10); even though they refused his advice, they soon discovered that his instructions were beneficial and crucial to their very lives (Acts 27:21-44). Because Paul held no malice against the Roman government even though they were oppressing and persecuting believers, he was able to receive benefits from the government and give his blessing to it.

The bottom line seems to be that we must have a pure heart to be able to influence the government. If our hearts are filled with greed, deception, or pride, then our motives and actions will be exactly the same as the men and women who have enacted public policy. In that case, we will not be able to bring any healing to the nation or its economy. Jesus taught us, "A good man out of the good treasure of his heart bringeth forth that which is good; and an evil man out of the evil treasure of his heart bringeth forth that which is evil: for of the abundance of the heart his mouth speaketh." (Luke 6:45) It is only if we have pure hearts that we can speak pure and godly counsel into the policymakers of our day. I encourage every Christian to take advantage of every opportunity he has to influence the government through casting his vote for honest candidates, making phone calls and writing letters and emails to men and women in office, and taking an active role in town meetings. He can also volunteer at his local political party office or candidate's campaign office when reputable candidates are promoting worthwhile causes. Furthermore, he can submit well-written and constructive editorials to the news media, post well-researched and logical blogs on the internet, and make constructive comments on websites, Facebook, tweeter, and any other social media. Additionally, he can provide his pastor with thought-provoking articles, books, and videos that can help him understand how he can play an important role by informing his congregation. But before any one of us can step into any one of these roles, we must thoroughly examine our own motivations. Anything done out of greed, the desire to gain personal recognition, the motive of stirring up trouble, or a vendetta against someone is a totally ungodly motivation that God cannot bless or cause to prosper. (Galatians 5:26, I Corinthians 13:1-3)

    Nathan pointed his finger into the face of the adulterous King David and point blankly accused him. (II Samuel 12:7) He could do so because he was a long-time trusted friend and advisor of the monarch. David listened because he knew that when Nathan spoke, he was doing so for the good of the king and his kingdom – not because the prophet had a personal grudge against the government or because he had a secret agenda that would bring him some personal gain. We, too, can blatantly point out the errors of the government if we have first – through our personal efforts and support of the government – won the platform from which to make such allegations. John the Baptist also fearlessly made boldfaced accusations against Herod the tetrarch. Even though the prophet eventually lost his head over these indictments, he was not immediately executed because Herod recognized his reputation as a prophet. (Matthew 14:5) Let's back up and see how John had gained such a reputation. Luke chapter three records that John the Baptist's message was one of financial integrity; he told everyone that they should share their clothes and food with those in need, he addressed the tax collectors by telling them not to oppress the citizens through collecting extra coins for their own pockets, and he encouraged the soldiers to be content with their wages and to not extort money from hapless victims. As an advocate for such simplistic but equitable reforms, there is no wonder that he gained the reputation of a prophet and had a stage from which to speak out against Herod's transgressions. The Old Testament prophets called the government "on the carpet" but also worked within the system to prove their loyalty and allegiance to the government they brought under their scrutiny.

The next step is to actually step up to the plate to execute change. Joseph intervened in the nation of Egypt at a time when the monetary system had failed. (Genesis 47:15) He prevented a national crisis by implementing a fair taxation program and a resource management system for the country. When he interpreted Pharaoh's dream to reveal that there were to be seven years of plenty followed by seven years of famine, he also added a divinely inspired proposal as to how to deal with what would otherwise be an inevitable economic collapse. He suggested that one fifth of the resources of the land be stored up during the years of plenty and then rationed out during the years of scarcity.

This was obviously a divine plan in that the math doesn't add up at first. Since there were to be only seven years of supply to sustain the people during the fourteen-year period, it would seem logical to store up half of the harvest during the first seven years in order to supply for the following seven years when there would be no income. However, Joseph had divine insight in human nature. He understood that if he taxed the people at fifty percent of their production, they would lose their motivation to work and would actually produce less. I personally witnessed the crippling effect of this sort of government-takes-all policy during the communism regime in Russia. When I visited Leningrad during the closing days of the communist era, there was no food on the shelves in any of the stores. The reason: under communism, the people said that the government pretended to pay them so they pretended to work. Years later, I revisited the city – now known as St. Petersburg – to find that it was a bustling and prosperous city under capitalism. Why? Because people never work harder than when they are working for themselves. Just like the lack of motivation under communism had paralyzed the USSR, so the lack of motivation brought on by too high taxes in Egypt would have essentially voided out the bounty that God was intending to give the people during the first period of plenty. However, Joseph understood that if he taxed the people at twenty percent, they would have enough left in their hands that they would be motivated to produce even more. To spell this principle out on a microfinance level, imagine that you can produce ten bananas and the government taxes you two of them. Looking at the eight bananas in your hand, you are likely motivated to try to produce twelve bananas the following year so that you will have ten left over when the government takes its share. The following year, you may be motivated to try to produce fifteen so that you'll have a dozen after taxes. It doesn't take an Einstein to see how Joseph's plan actually caused the nation to multiply its prosperity during the short window of opportunity that economists today would call a bubble market.

Before we leave Joseph, let's look at the internal aspect of this pure-hearted man. On several occasions, he had opportunity to take credit for his accomplishments; however, in each case he acknowledged that it was not his own wisdom or ingenuity that had been demonstrated. He gave God the total credit. When confronted with the dreams of the butler and the baker, he never claimed to be able to interpret them; he simply confessed that the interpretations of dreams belongs to God. (Genesis 40:8) When summoned to interpret Pharaoh's dream, he again gave all the credit to God. "God will give Pharaoh an answer of peace." (Genesis 41:16) Joseph accepted the position as Pharaoh's number one man, not because of his own ability, but because the Spirit of God was with him. (Genesis 41:38) Even when testifying to his own family, Joseph emphasized that it was God, not his own achievements, that had secured him the position as lord over all Egypt. (Genesis 45:9) We could simply sum up this point with the word "humility." Another significant characteristic we see about Joseph was that he was a man who never gave up his faith in God. He had more occasions than most to give up hope; yet, he somehow kept on trusting that God would do what He had promised. Certainly, the pit was a great place for him to throw in the towel – but he didn't. (Genesis 37:24) As a slave, Joseph somehow kept on believing that others would be bowing to him rather than his always being the one to kiss the dust before his Egyptian master. (Genesis 39:1) Just when Joseph had begun to feel that he was crawling out of his captivity and had become the master over Potiphar's house, he suddenly found himself in a dungeon. Yet, even in the prison, faith was still alive in his heart. (Genesis 39:20) When he saw a glimmer of hope as he sent the butler to Pharaoh with a message of his unjust imprisonment, Joseph found that he was a forgotten man with an unheard appeal. Nonetheless, he refused to give up his faith. (Genesis 40:23) One of Joseph's most important qualities was feeling. He never lost his sensitivity to others. Certainly, Joseph's life was full of tragedy and hardship that could have turned him heartless and callous to the world around him. But, his testimony bears no indication that he ever lost that cutting edge of gentle compassion. Genesis records that he wept (verse 42:24), that his bowels did yearn as he wept (verse 43:30), that he could not refrain himself as he wept aloud (verses 45:1-2), that he kissed and wept over his brothers (verse 45:15), that he wept for a good while (verse 46:29), that he wept at his father's death (verse 50:17), and that he wept when he granted final forgiveness to his brothers (verse 50:17). Never letting bitterness or hardness enter our hearts is one of the most important keys to positioning ourselves to influence others. Genesis 50:16-21 records one of the most moving stories in the biblical annals. It is the story of a man who has been hated, betrayed, and plotted against by his own brothers. After second thoughts on the scheme to murder him, they doomed him to the lowest station in life – that of a slave, a less-than-human piece of property to be used, abused, and misused at the whim of his master's will. Suddenly, these cruel brothers were confronted with the fact that this young lad is now their master and held their lives in the palm of his hand. One quick hand motion and their heads would be on the chopping block. Out of this macabre plot comes the most powerful statement of forgiveness ever spoken short of Jesus' own affirmation from the cross, "Father forgive them for they know not what they do." (Luke 23:34) Joseph's immortal words still ring with power millennia later as we read, "Ye thought evil against me; but God meant it unto good, to bring to pass, as it is this day, to save much people alive. Now therefore fear ye not: I will nourish you and your little ones." (Genesis 50:20-21)

    Three other examples of individuals who took up the challenge of political position in order to effect change were Nehemiah, Esther, and Daniel. Nehemiah stepped into the role of rebuilding the city of Jerusalem as it lay in ruins after the Babylonian invasions. He did so by acting on two levels. First, he used his influence with the king to gain accesses to resources (Nehemiah 2:8); next, he appealed to the average citizen to get involved in the project (Nehemiah 3:1-32). But let's look at his personal life to see what was working behind the scene to qualify him to bring about these great accomplishments. Like Joseph, he was a man of great sensitivity. Even though he was miles away from Jerusalem and in a secure position, his heart was "tuned inside out" when he heard about the suffering in his city. (Nehemiah 1:4, 2:3) Again, like Joseph, he was a man of faith who knew that God could and would act to correct the injustices against His people and that he (Nehemiah) could be an instrument in the hand of God as He was righting this wrong. (Nehemiah 2:20) In Queen Esther's case, she stepped forward to realign a major portion of the wealth of the Persian Empire that was being used to destroy God's people into funds in the hands of God's faithful servant. (Esther 3:9, 8:7) But the backstory to her courageous actions has to do with the change that took place in her heart to motivate her actions. Originally, she was interested simply in her own personal wellbeing – taking care of number one, as we say. (Esther 4:11) In fact, she was initially embarrassed by the fact that Mordecai was making a public display of himself, apparently sensing that his actions could eventually cause her to look foolish since he was her closest living relative. (Esther 4:4) However, the whole picture changed when she realized that God had placed her in a position of authority for the purpose of securing the good of the public rather than her own personal pleasure. (Esther 4:14) In fact, her heart was so changed that she became willing to take on a dangerous role that could cost her life. (Esther 4:16) Again, we see that the power of change that she exerted was a direct result of her godly heart. Daniel, like Joseph who took over the entire economy and monetary system of Egypt because of his supernatural wisdom that exceeded any other counselor's ability (Genesis 41:39), was also elevated to a position of national policymaking because it was obvious that he had divine wisdom and understanding (Daniel 5:11, 14). None of these individuals presented himself or herself as a raging fanatic touting conspiracy theories. They were all levelheaded individuals who knew how to present themselves politely, yet confidently, before the authorities and decision makers of the country. Because they knew how to fit in, they could be accepted in the halls of power. They were accepted because they cared for the people whose lives would be affected by the policies they were to enact. As the little saying goes, "No one cares how much you know until they know how much you care."

Jesus summed up the whole matter with one simple statement, "For where your treasure is, there will your heart be also." (Matthew 6:21, Luke 12:34) In both instances where He made this statement, He was speaking of laying up for ourselves treasures in heaven where they do not rust and decay like they do here on earth. It is obvious that the way He felt that we could accumulate investments in our heavenly bank accounts was through expressing charity toward our fellowman. Therefore, if our treasures are invested in other men, our hearts will follow our treasures – others. In other words, if our motivation for wanting to correct our nation's monetary policies is how it effects our own bottom line, then our treasure is still physical treasure. In that case, we will be tainted in both our motives and actions. In fact, we might even advocate unjust monetary practices as long as they bring us personal profit. On the other hand, if we have made our heavenly account the top priority, our hearts will follow our treasures – other people. The end result is that we will advocate and champion honest causes and equitable policies that bless others immediately and will set a course that will not implode upon itself, leaving destruction in its wake for any future generations.

Paul instructed us to pray for those in authority so that we can lead quiet and peaceable lives in all godliness and honesty. (I Timothy 1:1-2) He finished the sentence with the reminder that the prayers really are for ourselves in that the end result is that our own lives will become more peaceable. Every decision – right or wrong, wise or unwise – that our government makes eventually winds up affecting our personal lives. Therefore, it is only in our own best interest that we take the time and go to the effort to understand the policies and decisions being implemented on the local, state, and national levels so that we can intelligently pray for the men and women who make those decisions. We must pray that they will have the perception and integrity to make wise and honest choices.

One of the most moving passages in the Bible comes from exactly this seedbed. The prophet Isaiah was in deep intercession before the Lord after the death of King Uzziah whose very name meant, "God is my strength." During his fifty-two-year reign, this great man had brought Judah to one of the truly high points in her history. Prosperity, peace, advancement, surety, safety, strength, justice, and righteousness characterized this golden period. However, Isaiah knew the legacy that had developed: good king, evil king; prosperity, poverty; righteousness, idolatry. His nation's sordid history was as predictable as a yo-yo. As certain as it would go up, it would go down. The higher it would go up, the further down it would plummet. After reaching such a high point, Isaiah feared the rollercoaster ride down to the bottom that must surely await him and his people. In his quandary, Isaiah was forced to his knees to seek an answer from God. And the answer did come – that it doesn't matter so much who is on the earthly throne as long as we realize that God Himself is on the heavenly throne!

> In the year that king Uzziah died I saw also the Lord sitting upon a throne, high and lifted up, and his train filled the temple.

> Above it stood the seraphims: each one had six wings; with twain he covered his face, and with twain he covered his feet, and with twain he did fly. And one cried unto another, and said, Holy, holy, holy is the LORD of hosts: the whole earth is full of his glory. And the posts of the door moved at the voice of him that cried, and the house was filled with smoke. (verses 6:1-4)

Having mentioned the spiritual rollercoaster ride that Israel experienced with their mix of godly and ungodly kings, we would do well to take a look at the one king who seemed to be the best of both worlds – secular ruler and prophetic man of God. King David earned a place of distinction because he was a man after God's own heart. (Acts 13:22) As we have already seen, the heart of the matter seems to be the matter of the heart. Whether we desire to influence the governmental rule from without or within, we must do so with the right heart attitude. Therefore, it is no wonder that God specifically chose David over his brothers when He directed the prophet Samuel to go to Jesse's house to anoint a monarch to lead the nation. No matter what leadership potential the seer could discern in the other seven contenders for the throne, God declared that only David had the right internal qualifications. "But the LORD said unto Samuel, Look not on his countenance, or on the height of his stature; because I have refused him: for the LORD seeth not as man seeth; for man looketh on the outward appearance, but the LORD looketh on the heart." (I Samuel 16:7) Even though David ruled the nation with the authority of a powerful civil leader, his real strength lay in his sensitivity to and open relationship with God. He described his underlying formula for national government.

> Blessed is the nation whose God is the LORD; and the people whom he hath chosen for his own inheritance. The LORD looketh from heaven; he beholdeth all the sons of men.

From the place of his habitation he looketh upon all the inhabitants of the earth. He fashioneth their hearts alike; he considereth all their works. There is no king saved by the multitude of an host: a mighty man is not delivered by much strength. An horse is a vain thing for safety: neither shall he deliver any by his great strength. Behold, the eye of the LORD is upon them that fear him, upon them that hope in his mercy; To deliver their soul from death, and to keep them alive in famine. Our soul waiteth for the LORD: he is our help and our shield. For our heart shall rejoice in him, because we have trusted in his holy name. Let thy mercy, O LORD, be upon us, according as we hope in thee. (Psalm 33:12-22)

Notice that David described a two-fold criterion for a successful government: 1) The nation as a whole – especially symbolized by the government and particularly the king as the unique person of authority – has to be in right standing with God. 2) People as individuals must make a conscious choice for the Lord. The unfortunate reality is that it is possible for one but not the other condition to be in place. For example, a nation can adopt a very godly stance and put severe laws in place against prostitution; yet, if the people continue to have lustful thoughts even though they don't have occasion to act them out, God still holds them accountable for having committed adultery in their hearts. (Matthew 5:28) On the other hand, it is possible for the people as individuals to deliberately and obediently follow the Lord and still be hindered in obtaining national blessing if the nation as a whole is in disobedience. A classic example can be seen in the story of Caleb and Joshua; they were righteous and godly in their desires and actions, but the rebellion of the nation as a whole hindered them from entering the Promised Land for four decades.

(Numbers 14:33-34) Interestingly enough, this is one of the very few biblical examples of a democratic rule – where the vote of the majority overruled the leadership of godly spokesmen.

The bottom line is that a Christian nation cannot simply be one that is declared so on paper; it must be one in the hearts of both the leadership and the people. John Adams, the second President of the United States of America, apparently understood this truth when he penned the immortal words, "We have no government armed with power capable of contending with human passions unbridled by morality and religion...Our Constitution was made only for a moral and religious people. It is wholly inadequate for the government of any other." In other words, it doesn't matter what the constitution writers say on paper about a government; the real essence of any nation is determined by what is in the hearts of the people and their leadership. Thomas Jefferson, who not only followed Adams in the Presidency but was also one of the major contributors to the Constitution of the United States, clarified this truth even more candidly with his powerful observation, "The reason that Christianity is the best friend of government is because Christianity is the only religion that changes the heart." Now that we've quoted the second and third Presidents of the United States, let's go back and hear from the second and third kings of Israel. Solomon, Israel's third royal, affirmed, "Righteousness exalteth a nation: but sin is a reproach to any people." (Proverbs 14:34) David, the second to wear the nation's crown, attested, "Happy is that people, that is in such a case: yea, happy is that people, whose God is the LORD." (Psalms 144:15)

I know that it seems that we've strayed a long way from the constitutional rewrite in Zambia, so let's head back to Lusaka (the nation's capital) for just another few minutes. While the debate was underway in the legislature and among the citizens, one surprising turn of events developed – the advocates of an official declaration of a Christian nation received unexpected support from a totally unforeseen ally when the Muslim minority expressed their unanimous backing for the motion! To the Muslims, it was a "no-brainer." They were totally accustomed to and comfortable with the idea that a nation whose majority population is of the Muslim faith be officially considered an Islamic nation under the rule of sharia law. At least two dozen countries around the world today are officially Islamic nations, and many of them actually bear the title of Islam in their names. They unabashedly testify to the entire world that their foundational ideologies and ruling values come directly from their Muslim faith. For those who were accustomed to unapologetically taking a stand for their convictions there was no question that the Christian majority of Zambia should do the same.

My recommendation to the people of Zambia was that they shouldn't back down from proclaiming that they intend to base their nation on the only infallible source of values and ethic – the Bible. Furthermore, I commended them that they unashamedly proclaim to the world that they know that the only authority through which they can have a strong and peaceable government is through the practice of the Christian faith. However, my warning was that they never feel that simply writing the words into the constitution would be their "ticket" to a godly society or that they could expect the government to make the difference. No matter what the constitution says, it is always what each individual believes and lives by that will determine whether Zambia, the United States, Nigeria, or any country on earth is a godly nation. The real foundation for a nation is in the hearts of the people, not the documents in the statehouse. The real key is in the continual proclamation of and acceptance of the gospel: "I am not ashamed of the gospel of Christ: for it is the power of God unto salvation to every one that believeth; to the Zambian first, and also to the whole world." (My personal paraphrase of Romans 1:16)